For dear Estrellita &
Romeo
For lots of thanks
from our heart for giving
love to Mummy
Maya & Harish
June 1
2014

Metaphors of Healing

Playful Language in
Psychotherapy and Everyday Life

Harish Malhotra

D1453767

Hamilton Books

A member of
Rowman & Littlefield
Lanham • Boulder • New York • Toronto • Plymouth, UK

Copyright © 2013 by Harish Malhotra

First published in 2014 by Hamilton Books

Hamilton Books
4501 Forbes Boulevard, Suite 200, Lanham, Maryland 20706
Hamilton Books Aquisitions Department (301) 459-3366

10 Thornbury Road, Plymouth PL6 7PP, United Kingdom

Library of Congress Control Number: 2014933026
ISBN: 978-0-7618-6351-9 (paper : alk. paper)—ISBN: 978-0-7618-6354-0 (electronic)

∞™ The paper used in this publication meets the minimum requirements of American
National Standard for Information Sciences Permanence of Paper for Printed Library
Materials, ANSI/NISO Z39.48-1992.

Contents

Acknowledgments   v

Introduction   vii

The Daily Grind   1

Interpersonal Relationships   15

Problem-Solving   39

Beating Negative Thinking   57

Letting Go & Living Now   69

Know & Appreciate Yourself   81

Dating   91

Being a Better & Happier You   95

Working Toward Success   113

Mindset   129

Consideration for Others   145

Marriage & Romantic Relationships   157

Addiction   171

Connecting with Difficult Patients   175

Recommended Reading   181

Index   183

Acknowledgments

Dr. Salman Akhter has been a source of inspiration to write from my days of residency in Chandigarh, India. My wife Mahamaya has to bear the pain of listening to the first readings of all my lectures and writings. She has borne this pain with a smile and made my efforts worthwhile. Yashpal, the noted Hindi writer, was my uncle and he profoundly affected my early life. Anand, my cousin, has been encouraging me to write since I was in 9th grade. Mr. Bharat Chand Khanna, my father-in-law, was also a writer and I am proud of his literary work.

I would like to thank my wife Mahamaya, my children Gautam, Rahul, Monica, and Kavina who encouraged me to create YouTube videos. They were fun-filled family projects.

I want to thank my departed parents, Krishna and Sohan Lal Malhotra, and my brother Satish. They gave me a secure childhood where I could fantasize without fear of losing touch with reality.

My aunts Kamla and Shukla and my cousin Satinder had only one business on this earth. They came only to shower me with their love. My aunt Bimla and Uncle Gian Chand Khanna and Yashpal family gave me the absolute best summer vacations to play.

A plant in a greenhouse produces large flowers. They were the greenhouse and I was the plant.

I want to thank Dolores Lisooey, my office manager. She always gave her secretarial and English grammar help.

Ms. Jennifer-Crystal Johnson gave help from A to Z in the preparation and Ms. Laura Espinoza and Ms. Nicolette Amstutz of Hamilton Books in the publication of this book. I want to thank them.

Introduction

The idea for using metaphors came from my struggle to reach my patients in therapy. I tried to communicate an abstract concept, and as I struggled, out came a metaphor. "A-ha!" moments in psychotherapy are few and far between. When I used metaphors, I heard that "A-ha!" more often. The glimmer in the eyes of my patients was easy to see.

One of the criteria of scientific validity is reproducible results. A nurse told me that 20 years ago, she had heard one of my metaphors. I was talking to a patient who refused to take his medication on the psychiatric floor. I asked him, "If your house is on fire and the fire engine throws water on the house to save it from the fire, would you refuse the fire engine because of the water damage?"

The patient replied, "No."

I went on, "Your illness is the fire destroying your life. The medicine is the fire engine. The side effects are like the water damage. Would you refuse the fire engine and let the house be destroyed by the flames for fear of water damage?" The patient agreed to take the medication.

The nurse said that she had used that same metaphor over the last 20 years whenever a patient refused medication and it worked every time.

My patients frequently say that I have helped them through the metaphors. I used the metaphor of *Peeling Potatoes* with one of my patients. The next day, another patient repeated it to me. When asked, he said he had heard it in the Alcoholics Anonymous meeting next door to my office. It spread very fast.

I teach an open-ended interview technique to second year medical students. I use metaphors. I say that a closed-ended question is like throwing a line with a hook. It catches a single fish or answers a specific question. If they asked an open-ended question, it was like casting a net. They would be surprised by what they catch. In their feedback, they consistently appreciate my metaphors to help make learning easy.

This book can be used by psychotherapists to help them reach their patients. It can also be used as a self-help book. If you're struggling to understand an ailment or reach a patient, these metaphors can help you find your way.

More than anything else, they are designed to improve understanding and help people get through difficult times. Whether you're having trouble in relationships or just want to learn to be happier, *Metaphors of Healing* aims to guide, teach, and solve problems that all of us face on a daily basis.

My patients urged me to write a book with the metaphors that helped them, so I started collecting my metaphors over the span of 40 years. Here is the result, which I will now share with you.

Sometimes a picture or video is far easier to comprehend than the written word. I encourage the reader to experiment with creative ways of conveying the text to patients. I have personally enjoyed working with my family and friends on visually interpreting some of these metaphors in a series of videos entitled, "Helpful Hints for Your Hang-Ups." As of this printing, the videos can be found on YouTube at https://www.youtube.com/user/nanabhai/videos.

The Daily Grind

A TOURIST SEES MORE THAN A LOCAL

In the city of New York, tourists sit on the sidewalks with a tour book and a pencil in their hands, checking off what they are going to see that day. They visit the Empire State Building, the Statue of Liberty, the Metropolitan Museum, and Times Square. They look at the flashing neon lights and enjoy each moment because they have a limited amount of time to see it all.

However, people who live in New York walk around with cell phones plastered to their ears, never looking where they are going. A lot of them have never even been to the Museum of Natural History or the Museum of Modern Art. They have never stood on the corner to enjoy a hot dog with tangy ketchup. They have seen less of New York in their lives than the tourists see in days.

Some of us go through the same mundane actions, letting our life pass by. On the other hand, some of us come to this life not taking it for granted, knowing that death is around the corner, knowing that disease could affect us any time, and we want to enjoy it as much as we can. We live in the present, seeing as many things as we can.

Change your attitude from that of a New Yorker living in New York to that of a tourist visiting New York. You will get much more excitement and joy out of this life.

KEEP YOUR LIFE FILLED WITH FUN

It is not only important to mow your lawn, it is also important to plant flowers to make your backyard look beautiful.

It is not only important to do routine activities of life like work and household chores. Find time for your hobbies and time with friends to bring joy into your life.

WHAT IMAGE DO YOU PROJECT?

When you see a rattlesnake, you avoid it. You stay far from it and wouldn't even consider picking it up or you might get poisoned. When you see a bunny rabbit, it looks adorable and you would have no problems picking it up.

You have to decide what you want to look like. Both animals have their functions. If the environment is hostile and there are dangers around, being a rattlesnake is a good idea. If the environment is good and friendly, being a bunny is more appropriate.

The rattlesnake and the bunny don't have a choice to change their behavior. We human beings *do* have a choice to adjust our behavior to the situation. If you are scary to your family, like a rattlesnake, they are going to withdraw from you. You didn't want that. You have to be like a bunny with your family so that you and your family members all feel loved. But if something happens to threaten your family, it would be appropriate to turn into a snake to defend them.

Change your behavior according to the needs of the situation.

THE SCENIC ROUTE

A GPS asks for your destination first. Once it knows your destination, it asks for your preferences. Do you want to go through the highways or the scenic route? It charts its way and takes you there. If you make a wrong turn, it brings you back to your path.

In life, use the concept of the GPS.

Think of your destination first, i.e. professional success. Next, think of your preferences. What else is important to you? Do you want time with your family and time for a charity? Once you are clear, live your life carefully.

My wife chose to practice Psychiatry where she could choose her own work hours. She would drop the children off at school, go to her office, finish work in time, and pick them up. She moved her practice closer to our home and the school so that she was available if the kids were sick. We kept our lifestyle simple. We avoided expensive vacations and cars to decrease the pressure of earning more money.

We traveled in our life through a scenic route. You can choose to do so, too.

DRIVE EFFICIENTLY

If you have a limited supply of gas and a long way to go, please take precautions. Drive at a steady pace, go at modest speed, and do not accelerate and brake excessively. Look ahead and slow down without braking.

You do that in your life, too. Live at a steady pace. Go at modest speed. Do not make sudden decisions without thinking them through. Don't surprise others with sudden decisions made on impulse.

Look ahead and plan how you will deal with leaner times.

PHOTOCOPY OF YOUR DAY

You pick up a book to read. You find that the first page was interesting but when you go the second page, it is a photocopy of the first page. The third page is a photocopy of page two, and page four is a photocopy of page three. The fact is, all of the pages have the same thing on them.

Do you ever feel bored? You may be a person who keeps photocopying the itinerary of one day over and over. Keep a record of your daily activities. You get up at the same time, eat the same cereal, see the same friends, drink the same beer, and tell the same stories sitting on your favorite bar stool.

No wonder you start finding your life boring. You have become intellectually lazy. You do not put effort into doing different things every day. You make a photocopy of each day as it comes. There are no new people, restaurants, foods, books, or experiences to break your monotony.

If you want the book of your life to be interesting, write a new page every day. Don't be afraid of goofing up the story. Even if you find the second page to be less interesting, it will not be a repetition.

AN ORDINARY MASTERPIECE

I was visiting a friend's home. I saw a very colorful pattern framed and decorating their wall. It was so beautiful and colorful that I kept looking at it. It looked familiar, so I asked my friend about it. He said that it was a page out of his eight-year-old son's coloring book.

I recalled my own son's coloring books. He used to fill them up with crayons very quickly. We used to discard them. However, his son had done it so well that not only did it look exceptionally beautiful; my friend had framed it to decorate the wall.

We are all given a day made of 24 hours. We may fill it with lazy coloring, one or two shades—these are like mundane things in our days like sitting on the porch, watching TV, or sifting through junk mail.

We may also fill it with vibrant colors—worthwhile things like writing a novel, working for Red Cross, or going to visit family. Whatever we do, we are filling that page of life made of 24 hours. We can do it ordinarily or we can make a masterpiece out of an ordinary day, which will become a memory for ourselves and others.

It is up to you; how will you color in the canvas that is your day?

THE CAR GEARS

With the engine on, press the accelerator. The car makes a noise but does not move. Now put the gear into drive and press the accelerator. The car moves forward. Now put the car into reverse. This time when you press the same accelerator, the car moves backwards. What happens to the car depends on its gear's position.

The same is true for the mind and body. Effort and energy are like the accelerator. They bring movement to our mind and body. However, whether the movement is positive or negative depends on our self-talk and attitude.

During the morning rush to reach my office in time, I would pant with a strained face, palpitating heart, and adrenaline surging through my body. I worried that rushing under pressure and strain would surely give me a heart attack.

One day I said, "Oh, look, this is my power walk. God has given me a chance to have a brisk walk early in the morning. I am a sedentary person. This is great!"

I do not strain my face. My head is not down; my shoulders are not bent forward anymore. The fear of a heart attack left me. I walk now with a smile on my face. I look up and forward with my shoulders back and my chest out, like a happy soldier.

It is the same energy and movement. It is the same rush, but I feel happier now. My psyche has moved from the reverse gear into drive because of the simple statement, "This is my power walk in the morning."

Say something to change your mental gears the next time you are rushing too much.

DRIVING ON THE HIGHWAY OF LIFE

You travel in the left lane. You have to keep a minimum speed, watch speeding cars from behind, and worry about a speeding ticket.

The middle lane is the best. Flow with the traffic and reach your destination in time, singing your favorite song.

Drive in the right lane if you are a prince. You travel as slowly as you want to. You can enjoy the scenery. You can take exits to flea markets.

There is a fourth way. Get off of the highway and do not worry about driving.

In life, you meet deadlines, obey the boss, negotiate with customers, and earn a livelihood. That is the left lane. The drive is so tiring that you want to quit and get off of the highway altogether.

Instead of quitting the highway, come to the middle lane. Reduce your work hours or take on fewer responsibilities.

You want early retirement. Retirement from the job takes away the benefits of work. The money, friends, colleagues, socialization, and time out of your home are gone. Retirement can take away the motivation for daily structured work. My father stayed in pajamas all day after his retirement. He gave all his neckties to me, stating that he doesn't need them anymore. He would not shave because he did not have to go anywhere.

If you do not drive your car, its battery goes dead. Keep active and keep working. Select the right lane and work part-time.

If you hate your career or you have had enough of working, then quit the highway. Once retired, plan to travel, go to museums, and visit relatives.

HAPPY PEOPLE AND UNHAPPY PEOPLE

If a beggar becomes a prince, he is not guaranteed happiness.

You can be a happy beggar or a happy prince. Alternatively, you can be an unhappy beggar or an unhappy prince.

Happy people highlight goodness in things. Unhappy people highlight the negative in things.

If you want to be happy, start noticing positive aspects of what happens to you on a daily basis. Consider disappointments as part of day-to-day life. As the time passes, you will recognize that you are becoming happier. Your unhappiness will change for the positive even though your life circumstances remain the same.

Two people can go through the same life yet one is happy and the other is unhappy. Who would you like to be?

BACKUP GENERATOR

Hospitals use a backup electrical generator in case there is a problem with the electricity. On the other hand, people run around to find candles in their homes if it is dark. They should keep candles and flashlights handy.

Jacqueline has been arriving late to her office six or seven times every month because her infant son has respiratory problems. She has to find a babysitter. Her boss has been very understanding, but recently he reprimanded her.

Jacqueline is like a homeowner who does not keep flashlights or candles ready for when it is dark. She must develop a backup system because her son is going to get sick again. She must arrange for a babysitter instead of running late for work so often.

Do you have a backup generator in your life if it gets dark?

HOP AND STEP

Hop and step *into* or *across* a puddle, it is your choice.

A child may step into the puddle because it is exciting. The child does not realize that getting wet can make him sick. The immediate thrill of splashing water in the puddle is more important than the long-term effect of a fever.

An adult on the other hand will hop and step across the puddle to avoid the water getting into their shoes. Yet he can derive the pleasure of having successfully hopped across.

When life offers you a puddle, think wisely.

COVERING YOUR TRACKS

Some of us leave clutter wherever we sit. We study at the kitchen table and leave papers and pens. We take off shoes and socks in the living room. We eat and leave the dishes in the sink. We leave clothes on the floor. At work, we leave unfinished projects.

Others complain about us. These habits of leaving clutter wherever we go create more work for others. Family members yell at us and our colleagues resent us.

Whenever you get up, look around. If there is anything unfinished, complete it. If there is physical clutter, clean it. People will love you for that simple habit change.

Also look at any emotional clutter you've left behind. Apologize before you leave the office or before going to sleep if you have yelled, hurt someone with an impulsive negative remark, or offended someone. If you don't clean the emotional clutter, you will have to come to clean the clutter of bad emotions the next day.

ECHO

The world around you is like a hollow well. The well echoes back whatever you yell into it. If you scream, "Stupid," you will hear a voice call back, "Stupid, stupid, stupid...."

If you yell down into the well, "God bless you," you hear, "God bless you, bless you, bless you...."

If you observe that everyone is walking around serious and no one is smiling, ask yourself what you are doing. Is your face so serious that people around you are reflecting back your own behavior?

A person who says, "Hello," "Good morning," "How are you?" and, "Have a nice day," sees people smile back. Over a period, he trains others to smile. A time comes when they greet him before he greets them.

What is the world echoing back at you?

A DINGY BOAT IN THE SEA

"You can take this job and shove it,
   I ain't working here no more…."
It is a Johnny Paycheck song. It sounds very cathartic.

However, after Johnny leaves his job, where does the paycheck come from? Expenses and mortgage bills do not stop. Johnny jumped out of a bad job into the fire of unemployment and poverty. It becomes harder and harder for an unemployed person to find a job.

If you are in a sea on a dingy boat, do not jump out and drown because you don't like the boat. Wait for a bigger boat, a ship, or a shore before abandoning the dingy boat.

Don't quit a job on impulse. Start looking at other jobs first. Apply for a job if you find one. There are better chances that they will hire you if you already have a job.

Once you have the new job, then you may sing the song!

"You can take this job and shove it,
   I ain't working here no more…."

USE YOUR GPS SYSTEM

The user types in a destination and the GPS device will display the best route to get there. If you make a wrong turn, the GPS device will recalculate the correct route.

You have a GPS system in your mind: your ability to evaluate your actions. Listen to your inner GPS and reduce your weekend spree, Friday drinking, or time with your girlfriend. Always ask yourself, "What is my destination? Am I on the right track?" Let your mind's GPS recalculate your route so that you can reach your destination.

STAY ALERT

Drivers can have a gray out or fall asleep at the steering wheel and have an accident while on a long journey. Share the task of driving to prevent that.

Carry some candies, crunchy food, coffee, and soda. Listen to music so that you don't fall asleep.

On the highway of life, you can end up with a monotonous job and mundane chores. You may zone out and have an interpersonal accident—like an impulsive affair—or slide into depression, alcohol, or drug abuse.

To make the journey of life spicier, add hobbies like gardening, painting, exercising, or cooking. Enjoy yourself by dining out or going dancing. Consider taking an adult class or become a volunteer.

Munching on fun activities will keep you alert on the highway of life and prevent interpersonal accidents.

DECORATE YOUR JAIL CELL

Prisoners in a jail decorate their cells by putting pictures on the wall or scratching their names in the concrete. We have an inherent capacity to derive joy even in difficult times.

If you feel that you are a prisoner of a bad marriage, a bad job, or a bad relationship, and you cannot get out right now, learn to enjoy as much of it as you can. During this time, you can also continue to plan your escape. A time will come when you will be free. Until then, decorate your jail cell. Life is short. Don't put joy on hold for too long.

THE CROOKED PICTURE ON THE WALL

You are madly rushing out of the house to attend an important meeting. You notice a crooked picture on the wall. What do you do?

Keep your priorities straight in your mind. Some people will stop doing an important task and attend to unimportant details. It is like flicking a small speck of dust from your desk when there is a mountain of files screaming for your attention.

Take care of the important meeting and ignore the crooked painting on the wall.

YOU ARE LIKE A RACEHORSE

Racehorses are easily distracted and do not run straight. The horse owners found an easy solution for the horses' distractions. They put blinders on either side of the horses' eyes and now the horses can only see what is in front of them. They cannot see anything else.

Some activities or hobbies are probably distracting you. Accept that you, the horse, are not able to run the race. Accept that you need your own blinders so that other activities don't distract you. Put the blinders on by saying, "I am a racehorse; I cannot see these hobbies or activities. The only thing I can see is the straight road of my career."

Do not hear, see, or talk about what will distract you from your path.

Remember: you are a *race*horse!

WHAT IS ENJOYABLE MAY NOT BE BENEFICIAL

Taking vacations too frequently is expensive, makes you neglect your work, and will also become boring after a while. Taking vacations too frequently may also cause unhappiness through breaking the bank, neglecting those you love, or creating a numbness to the pleasure of change and life.

Vacations are good only if they give you infrequent breaks from your routine.

UNCLUTTER YOUR WORK LIFE

When your family or spouse needs you, you have no time or energy left for them. It may be something simple like getting your little son's shoes polished for his concert.

Analyze repetitive useless activities that wear you down.

Unsubscribe to unnecessary magazines and newspapers. Call mail order companies and ask them to stop sending their catalogs. Buy software that protects you from unsolicited email. Call and make your phone out of bounds for telemarketers. Screen your calls. Do not get up from your dining table to answer the phone.

Reduce the clutter and make time to listen to your family.

PRUNE YOUR PLANTS

Take two saplings and plant them in your backyard. Prune one of the plants and let the other one grow as it is. The pruned plant grows straighter and taller. The plant you did not prune grows and looks like a bush.

Let us look at our daily activities. We do things impulsively, play video games, hang out with friends, and drink more than we intended. That is the end of our day.

If we had turned off the television, planted the tomatoes, purchased the groceries, and made the appointment with the dentist as planned, we would have felt good.

Because we did not prune the activities, the day grew into an ugly bush of purposeless activities.

Prune the wasteful activities and focus on the planned ones.

YOUR ENGINE IS HOT

If you work nonstop for 12 or 14 hours, your stress level rises. Your engine overheats. You ignore the signs of stress like increased irritability, short temper, extramarital affairs, lack of patience, and an increased consumption of coffee, cigarettes, or alcohol. Finally, you have professional burnout.

When you drive your car too long in hot weather, its engine may overheat. If unattended, the engine can catch fire. Keep a watch on the engine light, stop the car, and let it cool down.

On the highway of life, listen to your mind and body. When you notice these signs, do something to cool your engine down. Cut down on your work hours. Delegate more. Change your job. Take a few days off and go on a vacation. Make a determined effort to change your lifestyle.

Cool it down!

HAVE YOUR PERSONAL QUIET PLACE

Billionaires and presidents have their summer getaways. They get away from all the crowds and the press.

You also need a quiet place where you can get away from the noise, the crowd, the movement, and the turmoil. Once I had a Christmas party of more than fifty people in my home. My wife, my kids, and I had been busy all day cleaning the house, preparing food, and decorating our main floor for the party. At 10:00 p.m. when the party was at its height with lots of noise and merrymaking, I felt overwhelmed. All the rooms, basement, and outside deck were crowded with guests.

I went into the bathroom. As I closed the door behind me, all that turmoil stopped. I sat on the toilet seat, as if the throne of a king. That place was very rejuvenating. After that, whenever and wherever I feel overwhelmed, I go into the bathroom and sit on the toilet seat with my eyes closed.

Remember! From now onwards, wherever you are, you should have your personal meditation throne, just a few steps away—the toilet seat!

BEHAVE LIKE A MATCHSTICK

Take a matchstick and ignite it. There is a flash of the burning phosphorus followed by the burning of the wood. Let it continue to burn, and as it nears halfway down, the flame starts decreasing. Before the flame reaches your fingers, it dies. This happens because the wooden end of the matchstick was treated with a flame retardant. It helps to avoid burnt fingers and accidental fires. Is that neat or what?

Your spending habits should be like the flame of the matchstick. When you have plenty of money, you have the right to enjoy it on lavish things just like the first flash of the matchstick. However, as the money becomes limited, watch your spending. Before you exhaust your savings, you should curtail your spending. The last unburned part of the matchstick represents the mandatory 10% saving out of your paycheck. This will prevent an economic burn out and not create interpersonal fires between the family.

IS THE LEFT LANE TOO FAST

I become very anxious when I am in the left lane. The cars keep tailgating me because my speed is slow. I accelerate, but I fear losing control. At that time, I switch to the center or the right lanes. Once there, I relax.

The same situation happens with our lifestyle. Sometimes we travel in the left lane of the highway of our lives. We are overly involved with our professional activities. We end up without time for our household activities, time to read to our children and to play with them. When we do spend time with our family, we worry about neglecting the professional activities.

All of us have the same 24 hours in a day. The president of the United States and the wino in the gutter have one thing in common: both have a 24-hour day. Your problem is not less time; your problem is too many things crammed into 24 hours. If you are anxious, slow down and change lanes.

THAT BAT!

Sometimes a piece of paper on your desk keeps "hitting your mind" every time you look at it. Maybe you have to ask a question from your insurance. You procrastinate, telling yourself, "I will do it later, let me finish the important stuff first."

I remember one night a bat kept hitting our window repeatedly. It was scary. I was afraid that it would break the glass pane and enter the house. My mother told me to switch off the light, which may have attracted the bat. We switched off the light and the bat went away.

As the days go by, that piece of paper keeps hitting you in the mind the way the bat hit our window. If there were many such pieces of paper, it would be like a flock of bats hitting your mind's window. The glare of procrastination is attracting them.

Here is an idea: switch off the light of procrastination and the undone work will disappear.

THE BRAIN IS LIKE A NOSE

Every nose has boogers in it. Have you ever known a nose without them? If you have, let me know. I have not seen one. However, some people have clean noses and some have dirty noses, depending on their personal hygiene.

In the same way, the brain is a thought manufacturing factory. It has all kinds of thoughts, positive and negative. The average person has about 70,000 thoughts in a day. Do not be upset by thoughts that are sinful, crazy, sexual, or aggressive. Let them come. All of us have similar thoughts. Accept them as part of your normal functioning.

Just like there are no noses without boogers, there are no minds without strange thoughts.

THE SWAN AND THE LAKE

A swan glides majestically on the surface of a lake. Have you ever seen one step out of the water? It is dry. The water never touches its skin. On the other hand, you throw in a towel and it absorbs the water and sinks to the bottom of the lake.

We human beings swim through the lake of life. Problems like fear, greed, pride, wants, danger, and anxiety surround us like water. We get very wet and fear drowning. When we step out of those situations, we continue to carry them with us; we worry and stay wet. For example, if I leave my job, come home, and bring problems of the job back home with me, I'm like a soaking wet towel.

Maybe we can learn from the swan.

When we walk out of our offices, we should leave our problems behind. When we walk out of our homes, leave those problems there. Focus on office problems in the office and home problems in the home.

GO WITH THE FLOW

Do not try to pass a car on the highway unless you have a reason for doing so. Even if you spend your entire journey passing every car you see, there will still be cars ahead of you and behind you.

Instead, learn to enjoy driving with the flow of traffic. Look at the scenery. Listen to music. Chat with your family.

If you spend your life's journey competing with your neighbors, co-workers, or siblings, you will see the same results. There will always be someone with a bigger house or a higher paying job. Learn to live and enjoy your life as it is. Enjoy your progress. Take pride in your work, your family, and your achievements without comparing them to others. Do not decrease your own joy by always finding someone who is bigger, better, or richer. Learn to enjoy the journey.

MISTAKE CLEANUP

You are in a restaurant and there are crumbs of bread on your table. The server apologizes for the mess and cleans up the crumbs. Now you can enjoy your dinner.

The same is true in our lives. As we go about our daily activities, we drop crumbs of mistakes, delays, and tantrums. These crumbs make the tables of our lives unpleasant.

Wipe up the spills quickly by recognizing your mistakes. Take steps to rectify the problem and apologize to those you hurt. By the end of the day, people around you will appreciate you in spite of your mistakes.

Interpersonal Relationships

TREAT THEM LIKE CIGARETTES

You realize that cigarette smoking is bad for your health. You decide to quit and move on with your life. Some people have done that very successfully.

However, you may have failed in quitting. The second strategy is that you reduce the damage. The damage is directly proportional to how heavy your smoking is.

The following steps can reduce your smoking and decrease the damage. Reduce the frequency of smoking cigarettes. Reduce how long you smoke. Reduce how deeply you inhale. Restrict the places where you will smoke.

By taking these steps, you can cut down the total damage to your health.

Now let us discuss human relationships. Breaking your relationships can be the best strategy when people at your job or in your circle of friends are harmful to you. You can move on with your life.

However, if it is your mom, dad, brother, child, or someone else you can't break a relationship with, it is a great idea to treat them like cigarettes.

Your relationships also have controls for you to tweak. It will make the relationship more enjoyable for both of you.

Frequency: Control how frequently you meet, phone, text, and give gifts.

Duration: How long do you meet, phone, text, email, and spend time together?

Intensity: What do you talk about? How do you speak to each other? What kind of language do you use? What gestures, compliments, and curse words do you use? Do you drink when you meet?

Places and events: Discriminate where you will go or where the trouble will brew. For example, events where there is prolonged drinking can inevitably lead to squabbles.

By looking at each of these parts, you can control your negative or harmful relationships just as you control your smoking addiction.

PUNCHING BAG

This is an example from a patient.

"I helped my daughter during her premenstrual tensions, pregnancy, baby care, household work, and financially. Yet at the drop of hat, she yells at me.

"She is very nice with others but shouts at me and my husband without any reservation.

"I know she is under a lot of pressure, but I am wearing down. She has no one to turn to except us. She has no support from her husband or his family. We feel trapped."

Have you ever gone into someone's basement and seen a punching bag hanging? What was your immediate impulse? When you were alone, you punched it.

Did you ever come across a ferocious dog? Did you go and pet it or stay away from it?

Your daughter yells at you even though you do everything for her. It is because you and your husband have a sign on your forehead: "I am a Punching Bag!"

Your daughter is a simple human being. She sees a punching bag and goes after it. Very natural!

You are so easily available to help her and give her money whenever she needs it. She has not developed any resources because you are like air which rushes in to fill a vacuum. You are her enabler and she depends 100% on you.

A woman who does not have well-to-do parents who are available all the time uses her mind to develop resources. She makes friends with neighbors to swap babysitting. She works out arrangements with her husband and his family to do things.

Be her mom and not a punching bag for her abuse. Everything flows from you to her including money, help, baby care, and love. You deserve respect. You cannot leave it on her to give it to you. Demand respect in words and behavior and she will give it to you. Remember: you are teaching her how to treat you by putting up with certain behaviors.

REEVALUATING THE PAST

This is another example from a patient.

"We were best friends for eight years. Jack started associating with drinkers, drug users, and bullies. He wanted me to come to their hang out. He wanted me join that crowd.

"I was very confused. Our relationship had deteriorated. There was no more common ground between us. Were those eight years of friendship a waste of time?"

Let's say that you bought twelve fresh bananas and ate eight of them. They were tasty. Now the remaining four bananas have turned black and have started smelling bad. What would you do with them? Throw them away or force yourself to eat them? You should throw them away.

What should you think about the eight bananas you enjoyed out of that bunch? Should you throw up the first eight because the last four went bad?

Well the eight years of friendship were like the eight good bananas. The last four bananas have rotted. Don't eat them.

This is also true about a husband and a wife who divorce after a wonderful initial relationship. They also wonder about the time they spent. Were those years a waste of time?

Don't judge relations *only* on how they ended. Judge them also on how much they enriched your life while they were good.

THE SALES CALL

Sales people do two kinds of work to make a sale.

The first kind is inner work. They collect addresses and phone numbers, bring envelopes, and take notes. They prepare what they will say and write. They do all sorts of things called "inner work" as preparation for their outer work.

The second kind is the outer work like advertising, phone calls, and talking to customers. The outer work pays because the sale is going to come from the contacts made.

We do inner and outer work in our day-to-day life as well. Inner work is our wishes and thought processes. We work on our lives from the inside by doing well at work, enjoying our hobbies, and planning for the future.

The outer work is saying hello to people, smiling, writing a thank you note or letter, calling your sister, walking over to your neighbor, or picking flowers for your mom.

Ask yourself how much inner and outer work you do for your life. Are you an inner worker only or do you reach out to loved ones, too?

The salesperson that also does the outer work is going to make the sale.

DON'T LET THE PAST STINK UP NEW RELATIONSHIPS

Let's make believe you are carrying a bag full of garbage with you all day. A friend invites you to dinner. You are so used to carrying the bag of trash around that you bring it to dinner with you. You are used to the stink. It does not bother you. Your friend, though, cannot enjoy dinner due to the smell. You cannot enjoy the evening with your friend and wonder why he or she was not fun today.

It would have been better if you had discarded that bag in a garbage can outside.

Now let's go to a real life situation. People have a really bad, rancid, and painful end to a relationship. They want to move on with their life. They meet someone new. They think that unless they talk about the garbage of their previous relationships, they are not being honest and will not feel close to the new person.

Most of the talk centers around how bad the other person was and how the other person hurt them. I feel that this is bringing trash to the dinner table. The one who brings the garbage is used to the stink and feels fine. The other person feels that it spoils the evening.

I believe that all of these things are important, but I recommend you leave them in the garbage can outside. Use a close friend, a therapist, or a psychiatrist and work on your pain.

Keep your new relationship clean and enjoy it for what it is.

REJUVENATE YOUR FRIENDSHIPS

There are gold finders who go to abandoned gold mines and find gold ignored, forgotten, or left behind by the original mine workers.

Maybe you have been out of touch with some friends. They are like abandoned gold mines. Surprise them with a call or a visit. They will react with surprise, joy, and gratitude for your initiative.

You can mine a lot of joy with those forgotten friends.

MISUNDERSTOOD ENCOURAGEMENT

A father told his son that his room was dirty. All of his clothes were on the floor. He told his son that when *he* was growing up he kept his room clean and well-organized.

The son felt criticized by his father. The father kept saying, "I am not criticizing you; I want to help you to be a better person. I love you. I am your dad."

Finally, the father said, "I am telling you about how my life was to show you a goal to achieve. My achievements are not a yardstick to measure your performance. My examples are not to say that you are failing, they are to point out where you may want to go."

Both of them calmed down. The father saw his hidden criticism and the son saw his own negative interpretation of his father's motives.

CHERRIES

Life is similar to a bowl of cherries. While eating these cherries, you spit out the seeds and enjoy the fruit. If you find that a cherry is rotten, throw it away. It is not mandatory to eat it just because it is in the bowl.

Similarly, enjoy everyone who comes into your life. Talk to them and relate to them. Nevertheless, if anyone makes you unhappy or has a negative impact on your life (like a rotten cherry), don't be afraid to reduce your relationship with them.

It is not necessary to relate to everyone with the same intensity, nor is it mandatory to be friends with everyone just because they're in the same "bowl."

BURNING A BRIDGE

During wars when our armies retreated, they burned the bridges they crossed so that the enemy could not follow them. That is a good war strategy.

Burning bridges *before* you have crossed them, however, is not a good idea.

The bridges I am talking about are your resources and strength. Our relationships with people around us are the bridges of our life. Doing and saying impulsive things to destroy and hurt the relationships is like burning those bridges. If you need them during difficult times, you do not have them because you burned your bridges.

When you perceive a wrongful act towards you, it may be your misperception of another's intentions.

Take your time.

Clarify what the other person says before you overreact and burn the bridge of your relationship. Tomorrow, if you need that relationship, it will not be there.

Don't burn your bridges—life is not a war.

NO TERMITES, PLEASE

If you want to damage my house, go ahead and break down a wall, but please don't put termites in the foundation of my home. If you break a wall, I can get it repaired. If you put termites in my foundation, I have no chance of recovering my house again.

If you are angry with me, go ahead and hurt my feelings. That is almost like breaking a wall. Your open anger is easily visible and understandable. I will make efforts to bring you around. My feelings will get back to normal after a while.

On the other hand, if you develop resentment towards me, it will work like termites in the foundation of our relationship. Your resentment will be silent, just like the termites. I would not know it is there. I would not be able to do anything about it. After a while, you walk away or explode with rage. You will leave me bewildered as to what happened.

Hurt me, but not our relationship by expressing anger or concern instead of burying it and letting resentment build.

DEFECTIVE BRAKES

When a driver brings a car with worn off brakes to the repair shop, he may complain about the quality of the brake pads. If the driver brings different cars with worn pads, the driver—not the brake pads—has the problems. He overuses the brakes and thus, he wears off the brake pads. The answer is to learn better driving habits.

Jenna complained that her son, Jack, stays away from her. He does not return her calls. What a thankless son he is. She sacrificed so much raising him. She complained that her other son, Richard, and her daughter, Monica, moved away without leaving a forwarding address.

Jenna should listen to her children. What is she doing that is turning them away? She must examine her expectations, her communication skills, and her behavior. Continuing to blame her children for neglecting her is not going to bring them back.

Complaining about the brake pads will not solve the problem of worn pads. Learning to drive well will.

YOU SAID, I HEARD

My wife phoned me. "Bring a potted little Christmas tree. We don't have time and energy to decorate a *real* tree." I stopped at many shops on the way home. Finally, I found a little one-foot tall artificial pine tree in a clay pot. I looked at it and felt my hard work had finally paid off. I put it in our foyer and called my wife. I stood there with my thumbs comfortably tucked in my belt. She came, looked at the tree, and said, "Didn't you hear me? I had said I do not have time to decorate a tree. This is not decorated. I wanted a tree I had seen in the supermarket with little ornaments on it." She walked away disappointed. I stood there frustrated.

My wife did not communicate her need for a decorated tree. I failed to understand her.

Complex emotional expectations can create misunderstandings. We don't communicate our needs for tenderness, intimacy, affection, and love. We quietly await the other person to understand and fulfill them. When we don't get what we secretly desire, we call the other person insensitive.

It can be the other way. Your loved one tells you to do something, but you don't think it is important. You think it is a ridiculous demand. You don't feel it fits your personality. Therefore, you don't do it. Men and women complain that their spouses make fun of their desires for closeness and intimacy.

Next time, verbalize your desire: be precise with what you want.

Also, when someone expresses her desire, listen! Don't make a spoof of it because it is not important to you.

BACKSEAT DRIVERS

When I drive, my wife or my son warn me if am approaching a red light at normal speed. If my car is swerving to the left, my wife nudges me. Mostly their warnings are unnecessary because I have seen the light and would slow down in one more split second. However, there have been times these backseat drivers have saved our lives.

Jack has been thinking very negatively about his financial future. Often he talks as if he would end up on the streets. His wife has to remind him that things are fine. She tells him about their friends who are worse off. He settles down when his wife reorients him.

Just as my wife is a backseat driver in my car, Jack's wife is a back seat driver in his life. By keeping a watch on his negative thinking, she brings him back to his real course.

Let your loved ones be your backseat drivers. Be patient with them even if they sound redundant to you now. You never know when they will save you from life's disasters.

Always listen to them but do what you know is right.

THE SINGLE ROSE ON TOP

You come across a large bush of leaves and thorns. On the top, there is a large, beautiful rose blossom. You stop for a second and admire the beautiful rose: "Look at that. It is so beautiful!" and then move on.

Please note that you did not say, "Look at that thorny bush. How ugly it is, and look how many thorns on it." Instead, you were focused on the beautiful rose on top.

Similarly, when you meet a person, focus on their positive qualities as you did with the rose bush. You can learn to ignore their character flaws and opposing opinions.

There are many situations where you may have to tolerate this person. A simple example is a friend of your best friend or a coworker. If you focus on the positive and appreciate it, the negatives will become tolerable.

DRY BALLPOINT PENS

Do you have a penholder full of ballpoint pens on your desk?

If you need to write, you pick up a few and find that most of them are dry. Won't if be better if you had two pens there and when those were running dry you pick up two more? That way the pens you have are the ones you write with confidently.

Some people keep making new friends and acquaintances and have superficial relations with them. They cannot give full attention to anyone because they have too many friends. If they need someone in difficult times, they can't find anyone to turn to.

It would be good to have a few friends and give your full attention to those few relationships. You nurture them; take interest in their work, profession, happiness, and sorrow.

You have few good friendships like the few working ballpoint pens. You can be confident in these few strong relationships.

AN IDEAL PARENT

A cocoon gives life, protection, and warmth to a helpless caterpillar.

Children need parental love, affection, and protection during their childhood. The caterpillar has to cut open the same cocoon to become a butterfly. If the cocoon is too hard, the caterpillar dies within it.

Just like caterpillars grow wings and cut open their cocoons, growing children challenge the value which helped them to grow. This is somewhat necessary to become independent.

Children can only become assertive young adults if their parents are protective like a cocoon but soft enough to cut open.

HOW TO GROW A PLANT

Just as a plant dies with excessive sunshine, shade, or water, relationships die with too many emotions, excessive closeness, and interpersonal interference.

The plant will flourish if given the proper amount of water, shade, sunshine, and care. Relationships and friendships thrive and rejuvenate again if you give affection, love, tenderness, physical touch, kind words, recognition, and thanks. Do them in the right proportions.

How much is the right proportion? You have to be watchful and pay attention to the other person's needs as well as your own needs.

DIMMER

Don't break relationships off completely when things don't go right between you and others. The world is not all black and white; there are many shades of gray in between.

There are two kinds of switches for a light bulb. One is an on and off switch. The other is a dimmer. You can set the light according to your comfort.

You can increase or decrease the following to set the relationship to your comfort level.

1. Change the frequency of talking, meeting, phone calls, invitations, and gifting.
2. Change the duration of how long you meet, talk, and interact.
3. Change the intensity: What you talk about and how you talk to each other.

Next time when you want to break your relationship with someone, consider modifying it. You can continue to enjoy the benefits of the relationship but cut down on the problems.

A SAFE DISTANCE BETWEEN CARS

Cars have more accidents on a fast highway when the distance between them is small.

Some people develop very close and intense relationships, resulting in frequent interpersonal flare-ups.

Keep a safe distance from the other cars. It saves you from hitting some-one if he suddenly brakes.

How do we keep a safe distance in a relationship?

Have your own friends, hobbies, and time with your family. Learn to drive so that you are not dependent on your spouse to drive you everywhere. Learn how to cook so that you don't die of malnutrition when your wife is sick.

The safe distance is not because of fear of intimacy, but to enhance the relationship through a sense of balance for everyone involved.

HOVER BEFORE LANDING

"I got married just to get away from my abusive father. The husband was also abusive so I got a divorce after my first child was born."

Imagine that you are part of an army offensive. You are flying a helicop-ter to an unknown Island. You have two choices.

Land wherever you find a flat area or hover over the land and see the terrain, the woods, the lake, the sea, and enemy camps. Once you have the big picture, *then* you decide where to land.

When you know the terrain, you have more options for survival.

Before making an important decision, take a good look; take your time. Hover over the choice's terrain. Examine positive as well as negative conse-quences of the choices and then make your decision. Don't jump into enemy territory without first getting to know the surroundings.

LEARN FROM THE DOG

Dogs accept people exactly as they are.

They sniff, lick, bark, and jump to show their joy. Dogs return love endlessly.

No one likes to feel judged. The reason why a dog is called "man's best friend" is because a dog does not judge. He just gives his master love and affection, as long as his master is also good to him.

You can also learn to accept people, their personalities, and their deficien-cies. You can behave similarly to the dog when it comes to others in your life, as long as they don't take advantage of your treatment of them.

A KNIFE IS BETTER THAN ACID

A sharp knife wound bleeds at first and then heals. However, a scar created by an acid burn is ugly and disfigures a person for life.

In life, expressed anger is like a cut with a sharp knife. It is hurtful, but the person learns to deal with the hurt and is able to heal relatively quickly.

On the other hand, sarcasm and being passive aggressive is like acid. Sarcasm is underhanded anger. The digs veiled in supposed humor hurt the other person. When they want to clarify the issue, you say, "Don't worry; I was joking." The issues remain unresolved, resulting in the slow death of the relationship.

When you have a problem, don't roll your eyes. Talk about it calmly and with an attitude of solving the problem.

BEADS ON A NECKLACE

A necklace has beads, gold, pearls, trinkets, stones, and plastic. The things on a necklace have one thing in common: they all have a small hole for the string. There can be so many odd beads in a box, every one of them different. Nevertheless, the minute you fill that hole with a string, they become part of a necklace.

Rich people, poor people, small people, tall people, beautiful people, and ugly people all have an empty hole: a need to be loved and accepted.

It is the love and acceptance by fellow human beings that works like a string. We create a necklace of relationships the moment we fill that hole of need.

When you meet someone, remember the little hole in both of you, the need to be loved and accepted. You have the string of love and acceptance to connect with others.

EMOTIONAL ECONOMICS

Successful businesses have realized that if their representatives lend an ear to the complaints of their customers and help solve problems, the customers are more satisfied. The customer goes home happy because he feels heard.

Listen to the people in your life with all your attention, eye contact, and patience. Repeat what he or she said to make sure that you heard right. Let them know that you got it right. If you agree, it is ok to finish the argument by saying:

1. OK, sure.
2. I am sorry.
3. Thank you.
4. I heard you. I will take care of it by tomorrow evening.

Practicing this kind of emotional economics will help you maintain happy and healthy relationships with others.

DON'T REPLACE BROKEN GLASS WITH PLYWOOD

My brother-in-law was sitting in his garage-turned-family room. There was a window with six glass panes. He noted that the glass in one of the panes was broken. He replaced the glass with a piece of plywood in order to save money. After a few days, another pane broke and he replaced it with another piece of plywood. The more panes he replaced, the darker the room became. After a while, he decided to replace the broken glass with new glass. His garage filled with sunshine once again.

Suddenly he realized that the relationships with family and friends are like the windows of life that let in the sunshine. If we close these windows, there is darkness in our heart. For a while, he had "shut off" his relationship with his sister and brother-in-law because of mutual differences.

He called his sister and brother-in-law after two years of silence and initiated the relationship again.

We must work hard to repair a damaged relationship, and we cannot simply try to replace glass with plywood; we cannot replace certain people with other people.

STORING GASOLINE

Your neighbor leaves a free can of gasoline at your house. You store it in your garage. Now your house becomes a fire hazard. In the case of a small accident, your house could blow up. *Use* the gasoline; don't store it.

When someone makes a remark that irritates you, he has handed over a gasoline can to you. If you don't take care of the anger through discussion or forgiveness, it is going to accumulate in you. One day, a small incident is going to ignite your anger and a big explosion will destroy your relationship.

Don't store grudges inside. They will make you a ticking gasoline bomb.

LEARN FROM THE GPS

I have a GPS system in my car. It guides me in a female voice while I drive. I affectionately call her Mary. I have learned a lot from her.

Even though she is installed 24/7 in my car, she doesn't offer help unless asked. I have to key in my request before she gives me advice.

She needs to know exactly where I need to go in order to help. If my address is incomplete, she asks me to clarify the destination.

She also wants my preferences of highways verses scenic routes.

Once she is clear about my destination, she gives me clear and precise directions, one at a time. She doesn't overwhelm me with suggestions.

She watches where I am and tells me what the next step is. If she is thinking, she tells me so.

If I make a wrong turn, she doesn't criticize me for my mistakes. She does not mutter, "I told you so!" She recalculates where my car is and guides me.

She has a calm voice. Even if I am in a hurry and sweating with anxiety, her voice remains calm and collected.

That is what to do with your loved ones. Become a GPS in their life.

THE ICE CUBE

An ice cube has three specific states. Let it sit on a plate and it turns into a small puddle of water. Overnight it will evaporate, leaving no sign that there was ever an ice cube.

An argument between two people is like an ice cube. People are sure about what they said and meant. Yet, with time, their viewpoints soften like a melting ice cube. Their priorities change. When you meet them later, those differences have evaporated.

People don't realize that what is important today may not be so tomorrow. Do not aggravate yourself about an adverse opinion. The warmth of time will melt your opinions as well as your partner's opinions like ice cubes.

Views change with time. That knowledge will make you more tolerant of others in the long run.

THE COUNTERFEIT COIN

No matter how you look at a counterfeit coin it will remain worthless and fail to be accepted as real. Soon, it will be tossed in the junk pile or the trash and someone may even go to jail over it.

Our friends are also genuine or worthless.

When you first meet them, they seem wonderful. When you deal with them, you find that their value system is hollow. As you get to know them more and more, you can see just how hollow they really are. Maybe they're manipulating you to do things you normally wouldn't do; maybe they use you for something you have that they want. In any case, their friendship is self-serving and not genuine.

Distance yourself from them. A counterfeit that is masquerading as a real coin will not buy you a meal when you are hungry. In the same way, these fake friends will leave you when you are in trouble and in need of help.

It is better to have an empty pocket rather than having a coin that isn't real. It is better to have no friends than to have a friend who will abandon you when you need help after taking advantage first.

TREE OF FRIENDSHIP

Friendship is like a tree. It starts with a seed: a smile, an introduction, or a handshake. It needs care and nurturing: phone calls and meeting for lunch or coffee. Visit when there is a happy occasion or a sad event. You nourish the friendship with jokes and laughter.

You enjoy the fruits and flowers of good times and memorable moments. The tree can live a lifetime, giving you shade and protection from the oppressive heat of loneliness.

On the other hand, you can cut down a tall tree with an axe. Hurtful words or actions cut to the core of the other person. The tree of friendship can also get termites: festering doubt, mistrust, or resentment. Before you know it, the tree falls to the ground, leaving you friendless.

Nurture the friendships you value. Don't let chores and routines take precedence over your relationships. Likewise, don't let careless words or actions destroy what you have spent such a long time nurturing.

THE LUXURY OF STAYING ANGRY

Jack was worried about his grown daughter who had recently become very angry. Every time he tried to open a dialogue with her she would say, "Not now, Dad, I am not ready." He sent her emails but she did not respond, or she would respond with a short, curt reply. In short, she was angry and he felt helpless. He was getting more and more frustrated because he didn't understand why his daughter was so angry with him.

Jack had passed through a severe depression during the time that his daughter was in her teens. Jack's wife had died, leaving his daughter to take care of him while neglecting her own life.

It made sense to me. The daughter had been so busy taking care of Jack during his depression that she had no time to express or work through her own anger and resentment towards him. He was always on the verge of crumbling and the daughter felt that she did not have the time to work through her own grief.

Now that Jack is stronger again, his daughter is finally able to be angry and work through her own emotions. I told him, "Let her *enjoy the luxury of being angry* now that she can afford to. She will calm down in time. Meanwhile, wait patiently for her the way she did when you needed her."

Once Jack recognized it, he became more patient with his daughter and stopped reacting to it with guilt and impatience.

THIS WITHOUT THAT

Jan wants to see her granddaughter but she hates Sue, her daughter-in-law. Jan wants to meet the child without Sue, who refuses to let her child go alone.

I told Jan, "You tolerate the thorns on the stem of a rose because you value the bloom on top. If you break the rose away from the stem, it dies." The baby is like the bloom and Sue is like the stem covered in thorns.

She had to accept Sue as part of the baby. She had to open her heart to *both* of them.

DEALING WITH A TANTRUM

During a temper tantrum, people complain, yell, cry, and berate you for your wrongdoings. It is an upsetting experience. Habitually, we reflect their behavior by yelling and screaming back. Or else, we go into apologizing or getting defensive. These reactions aggravate the crisis.

Here is a technique that can help you deal with a tantrum.

Immediately make believe that the person who is throwing a temper tantrum is a two-year-old child. Make believe that you are a parent who fully understands the transitory and dramatic nature of the event. Remain relaxed. Keep eye contact with him. Nod your head in affirmation that you are listening. As long as your mental image of them is that of a child throwing a tantrum, you will remain very calm.

Once you've done this, summarize what they said calmly. Ask them if you understood them correctly. Ask them what they would like you to do to rectify the situation.

Often, you will get lucky and receive a logical response.

Later, you will likely hear a thank you from that person or someone who watched you handle a crazy situation so well.

THE ORANGE CONE

Always carry an orange cone or flares in your car. If your car ever stalls on a highway, place the cone about 200 yards behind it to warn others. The oncoming traffic can usually see your disabled car and will not hit you.

If you are in a bad mood, place an orange cone to warn others to avoid an interpersonal accident.

It is important to say, "I am under the weather. It's not you, it's me."

Once people know that you are feeling bad, they can understand you better and don't overreact or take your mood personally.

THE ROSE BUD AND THE THORNS

When your boyfriend gave you a long stem rose, you held it cautiously. You knew there were thorns on the stem. The thorns did not stop you from enjoying the fragrance and the beauty of the rose, though.

The same is true about others. With one wonderful quality, they possess ten irritating habits. That should not discourage you from enjoying someone's good qualities. You hold the long stem carefully to avoid the thorns. Handle others' irritating habits carefully; handle them so that you can enjoy the positives.

If you started discarding roses because of their thorns, there would not be a single rose you could enjoy. If you broke off your relationships because of their irritating habits, you would have no friends and family left to enjoy.

DEFECTIVE PHONE

Let's say you were calling your friend. He was asking you for certain information. You told him what you knew. He kept asking you the same question. You thought that the phone was defective so you started shouting. Does this sound familiar to you?

When someone responds inappropriately, we think that he did not hear us. Our tendency is to raise our voice. We think that shouting will make the other person understand us. We forget that there are many other reasons why people do not hear us.

Before you start yelling, ask yourself, "Will my shouting yield results?" If you think that deafness is the reason the other person responded the way they did, then go ahead and yell. You may or may not achieve the results you want.

If the problem is not deafness, then your yelling will not produce any results. It will only make your throat hoarse. Think about a different kind of reasoning that may work.

Listen to them again to figure out if *you* understood *them* right.

Think of strategies other than yelling.

HEROIN TO AN ADDICT

Your friend tells you that he is going through a withdrawal of heroin. You run to the street corner and bring heroin for him. The more you give him the worse he becomes. The best solution would have been to sit next to him while he went through his painful withdrawal and help him work through it.

Now bring the same enabling behavior to the addiction of reassurance. Martha tells Tom, "I don't look good." He says, "You look beautiful." The more Tom tells her that she looks good, the more she needs him to tell her that she looks good because Martha believes that she is ugly.

The answer to her statement that she does not look good is to say, "What makes you think that you do not look good? What can you do to look better?" Alternatively, "It must feel terrible to feel that you are heavy. What are you going to do about it?" You could also say, "Take the compliment and say thank you instead of negating it, even if you disagree."

Do not feed poor confidence with praise when someone depreciates herself constantly. The only person who can really change that self-perception is her.

PLUCK ALL THE BLOSSOMS

When you go for a hike in the woods, you see weeds and wild flowers. What do you bring home, weeds or flowers?

When you relate to someone, it is like going for a walk in the woods. You have no idea what you will see. Listen to him and watch him carefully. Every person you meet has good qualities (blossoms) and bad habits (weeds). He may have a lot of quirks and irritating habits. Ignore those. You don't want to pluck the weeds, right?

When you walk away, only take the positive, beautiful blossoms with you.

A BEAUTIFUL LAWN

You can go two ways if you want a beautiful lawn. First, focus your attention on the crab grass and dandelions. Work on each weed. After that, you will notice that there will be bald spots in your lawn where the weeds had been. Even though you removed all the weeds, your lawn still isn't as beautiful as you want it to be.

The second is a proactive method. Spread grass seeds all over your lawn, then add lime, weed killer, and anti-fungal medicine. Soon, you will have the beautiful lawn you wanted. There will be occasional dandelions, but a beautiful and lush grass will hide them.

Similarly, you can sort out your relationship problems in two ways. First is to focus on your defects and correct them. It is difficult to get those negatives out. They have deep emotional roots. Even if you take them out, they can return. The second way is planting positive things. Start taking care of each other. Do little things to please each other. Add new hobbies that you can do together. Take dance lessons, go on weekend trips, or join adult education classes together.

Lo and behold, you will begin to notice that your interactions are enjoyable again.

THE PILLOW FIGHT

When an argument ensues, both participants respond to each other's comments. It will not stop. Each person considers the other person to be argumentative. The real fact is that arguments happen between *two* argumentative people.

How can you stop the argument?

Visualize that you and I are in a pillow fight. I throw a pillow at you and you throw it back at me. This goes on for a while.

Eventually you get tired of this game. However, each time I throw the pillow at you, you catch and return it while telling me to stop it. I want to continue playing. Therefore, I throw the pillow back at you.

Here is how you stop.

When I throw the pillow, you catch it and keep it. You do not throw it back.

You say, "We are getting into an argument. Let us stop it here." You may choose not to respond to my comments. You may say that my facial expressions and aggressive body language are scaring you. You may excuse yourself. You may get me involved in a topic that interests both of us. You may suggest that both of us go and see a movie.

I will throw many pillows for you to respond to. If you do not throw them back, I cannot continue the pillow fight.

THE DECOR OF A HOTEL ROOM

When you arrive at a hotel, they assign a room to you. You stay in it for a few days and then move on. Sometimes you like the décor of your room, and sometimes you do not. If you do not like a painting on the wall, you do not call the manager to complain about it. As long as the bed is comfortable, the toilet flushes, and the shower works well, you are happy. You think that you are going to be out most of the day and come to the room at night to sleep only. Why bother complaining?

You come across many people in your life. Many of these relationships are transitory: your acquaintances, neighbors, co-workers, and even some relatives. All of them have their own quirks, their own likes and dislikes, which may clash with yours. With time, these little nuisance factors will go away.

It can be very energy-saving to accept these quirks as variations of life rather than to react with anger, frustration, resentment, agitation, or irritation.

Look at it from the other side. *You* have flaws from their point of view, too.

When you are spending time with someone, do not attempt to change their habits (the décor of the hotel room). Enjoy their company instead (the comfortable bed and warm shower). One day we all have to move on anyway.

THE PLANT IS DYING

You notice wilting, pale leaves and stunted growth in your plants. You throw the plants out and replace them with new ones. After a few days, you repeat the same actions. Finally, you ask yourself: what is the reason for the death of your plants?

Upon closer inspection, you find out the reasons. You have not watered them regularly. There was too much sunshine, too little shade, and no stake to support the plant's tender stems.

You decide to change your gardening habits. Like a good gardener, you make sure to water, prune, and fertilize your plants. You give them the sunshine and soil they need. You support the plants with stakes to hold them upright so that they can grow well. The plants reward you with beautiful blooms and green foliage.

Your relationships are different plants in your life's garden. Attend to everyone's needs individually. Each one needs a phone call, an email, a smile, or a hug. You will be amazed to see that the time spent on them will have your relationships blooming in vibrant colors.

If you pull up a plant in your eagerness for it to grow taller, you will pull it out of the soil. Its roots will wither and die. Similarly, do not raise your expectations from your relationship before it matures. The pressure to make a relationship grow faster will kill it.

STORE CHEMICALS IN AN AIRTIGHT BOTTLE

Your friends, Joe and Mary, are married to each other. Mary phones you about the injustices, cruelties, and emotional turmoil Joe has caused her. She has hated him for years. She tells you the choice words that Joe said about you behind your back.

She spills all that acid in your ear. Anytime you intervene or explain, it fuels her to reveal more malice about Joe. You walk away with a bottle full of the acid that she just poured in your heart and soul.

Before you recover, Joe calls you, screaming at the top of his voice. He tells you a long list of mean things Mary did to him. He is in total disbelief and wonders how she could do and say such nasty things. He is sick of her duplicity and manipulation. He also tells you some of the choice words that Mary said about you behind your back.

Both of them are close to you and you are aware of their strengths, weaknesses, and sacrifices. Both of them are correct and both of them are overreacting to the crisis.

Now you have two bottles of caustic chemicals just waiting to spill.

Keep the bottles airtight. *Do not tell either of them what the other said.* When you mix these two bottles of chemicals together, there could be an explosion. Do not try to mediate right away. If you do, both of them will automatically consider you to be in the opposite camp. They will misinterpret any information you reveal despite your best motives. They will also blame you for breaking their trust.

Let the chemicals in both bottles simmer down and cool off. Until then, make sure that those bottles remain airtight. Keep their secrets in your heart. Do not divulge them.

FOLLOW AT A DISTANCE

You have a friend who is unsure about directions to a destination, so you try to give him directions. He remains anxious about it, so you tell him, "Just follow behind me as I drive there."

Somewhere along the way, he follows you too closely because of his anxiety of losing you. You brake to avoid an accident. He bangs into your car because he was following too closely. Now he gets mad at you because you applied the brakes suddenly.

A driver who drives at a distance is good a driver. The one who tailgates is the bad one. Safe drivers keep their distance and avoid accidents.

Some of us are level-headed and competent in professional settings. They operate very well on the job because they know how to keep their distance with colleagues. They are keeping good distance to avoid emotional collisions.

However, when they relate to their friends and family, their emotional distance becomes so close that they become dangerous.

How do they become too close on the highway of life? They habitually vent about their fears, jealousy, anger, and conflicts with their dear ones. That generates further fears and conflicts in people close to them. If they habitually complain, it simply drags everyone's mood down so no one wants to be around that person.

People end up arguing, yelling, screaming, or even hitting. It is like having an interpersonal "car accident."

It will serve you well to keep your safe distance and avoid emotional collisions.

BE LIKE A SOAP DISPENSER

There are soap dispensers on the wall in a restroom. Press the plunger and it releases just enough amount of liquid soap to wash your hands. The soap will wash but there is no extra soap left in your hands. A defective soap dispenser will drip soap all over your hands and the bathroom floor. People throw away leaking soap dispensers.

You have to be like a good soap dispenser with your suggestions, advice, and criticisms. Keep them to yourself unless asked. Do not keep leaking soap and telling people what they should do. They will discard you if your advice leaks out constantly.

Be precise with your advice when asked. Do not overflow and dribble your suggestions all over others' precious time. People do not like to hear lectures about what they are doing wrong or how to live their lives.

TRAVEL LIKE A SNAKE

Have you ever seen a snake slither? If it encounters a large rock, it goes around it. If there are pebbles, it crawls over them. If there is a tunnel, it goes through it. Snakes can travel miles without moving or disturbing anything in their way.

Relationships are like jungles. Some of us have that wonderful quality of the snake. We can survive in these relationships by changing our style in dealing with people who are as stubborn as a rock. Try as you may, you will not be able to change their opinions. Some people are like pebbles or sand. They have no clashing opinions at all.

Think of how the snake makes its way: be ready to adjust to hurdles along the way and keep moving forward.

DON'T BE A LOSER

Losers are those who lose relationships in their life.

I know of a man who divorced his wife, yet her brother continued to like him. The man borrowed money from his brother-in-law but refused to repay him. His brother-in-law does not like him anymore. He got into a couple of business relationships but said nasty things to his partners. He told them, "I do not need guys like you in my life." Over time, he alienated more and more people. He has some money but he does not have any well-wishers now.

He is a loser.

In olden times when armies marched, they burned whatever they did not need. However, they also could not use anything if they had to return that way.

It is not necessary that you get along with everyone, but expressing unbridled anger through your words and actions results in burning your bridges. It pays to remain civil and keep good relations, even with those you do not need anymore.

You never know; you may one day need those who seem useless to you now.

EVERY COIN HAS TWO SIDES

A coin has two sides. We call them obverse and reverse. They coexist and form the coin as a whole. Similarly, human relationships also have two sides. Opposites coexist in human relationships just like the two sides of a coin.

When two people live together, they have likes and dislikes. To resolve these differences, they have discussions. Sometimes these turn into arguments. When you are going through a bad phase in your relationship, only the unpleasant side of the coin is visible to you. Remember that the positive side is hidden from you at that moment but it still exists.

Do not be afraid of the negative side of a relationship. That is simply the other side of the coin.

THE ASSUMPTION MONSTER

Many times, we start to worry about what people think or say about us. We conjure up a tangled web of assumptions about others. We fear rejection and retaliation.

Think of a little boy who draws a picture of a scary gorilla and then becomes frightened of the picture he drew. He refuses to enter the room where he hung the picture. He forgets that he himself drew the picture and that he has the power to tear it up.

When we make assumptions or fear people without good reason, we're painting scary gorilla pictures and taping them on other people like masks. The other person has no idea about the scary picture we painted of him. He is not aware of our fear or assumptions.

If the boy who drew the scary picture tore it away, he would not be afraid anymore. You can also visualize in your mind that you are literally tearing down the scary picture from your wife, boss, customer, or friend and see the real person that is right behind the scary picture drawn by assumption.

Recognize your fears and see the reality. Reality is always less scary than your fantasy.

POLISHING NEW RELATIONSHIPS

Starting a new relationship is like finding an uncut diamond. It looks like a piece of glass. If you throw it in the garbage can, it will become part of the garbage. How much the diamond sparkles depends on how much hard work and time goes into cutting and polishing it.

Your new neighbor, new girlfriend, new wife, or child is an uncut diamond. How these relationships will turn out depends on how much time, thought, and effort you have put into them.

Continue polishing your relationships and they will sparkle.

THE TWO SIDES OF EVERYONE

A rose is beautiful and smells great, but watch out for its sharp thorns. Hold the stem, aware of its thorns, and enjoy the rose.

People are like the rose. They have good and bad qualities. You can enjoy their positive qualities if you carefully bypass their negative ones.

My beloved cousin used to get drunk after 7:00 PM. I used to meet him before his drinking time. We got along well for many years.

Recognize the negatives, but circumvent them and you will enjoy the beauty of the person.

TREATING EMOTIONAL BLEMISHES

Do you remember getting acne? Remember how ugly and painful it was? One day you saw a white head. You washed your hands and face with soap and water and squeezed it. Ouch! It was painful. But the healing started and your skin looked smooth again.

Every now and then, a hurtful word is spoken, an action is misunderstood, or a birthday is forgotten. A problem becomes an ugly blemish of misunderstanding. You are constantly aware of the pain and anguish every time you think about it.

To start the healing process, ask for a few minutes of uninterrupted time in privacy with the one who hurt you. Make sure that you are not hungry, angry, hot, in a hurry, or needing to go to the restroom. You feel relaxed, less defensive, and accept your faults.

Bring up what you want to say. Start with an, "I feel...," statement. Express your genuine need to resolve the issue, apologize, and move on. Once you have worked out a solution, the blemish will begin to heal.

Problem-Solving

PLANE, CONVEX, OR CONCAVE?

There are three kinds of surfaces.

Things stay on a plane surface for some time and then go away after a while. Convex Surfaces do not collect anything. You put them in the rain outside and everything slips off of them; they remain dry. Concave surfaces collect whatever falls on them. If you leave a concave surface like a saucer outside in the rain, it will be full of water.

Some people are like convex surfaces. Whatever problem comes, it slides off of them and they remain dry. People complain about their insensitivity. On the other hand, some people are concave. They collect problems, even the smallest ones. They are like a plate collecting rainwater and they do not let the water go. The water stays until it stagnates. They keep on worrying about whatever they collected.

They have a habit of collecting the negative things that happen to them and they don't let it go, so they become negative and wallow in complaints.

Do not be insensitive to others' needs like a convex surface. Do not collect stinking water like a concave surface. Instead, be more like a plane surface: decide what should stay with you and what should not.

DON'T IGNORE THE PROBLEM, HANDLE IT

If your sofa rips open and a spring is sticking out, you either have to fix the sofa or replace it with a new one. If you don't, the spring can cause injuries to you or your family and friends. Either fix the spring or get rid of the sofa.

The same thing goes for relationships. If you have a relationship with someone and see problems developing, it would be a good idea to talk about the problem, try to find a resolution, or go to therapy for help.

If you still can't fix it, maybe it's time to replace the sofa so no more injuries are caused by something broken.

RATS

Set up traps as soon as you see rat droppings. You don't have to wait to see the rats to take action; you are taking early action.

In life, also keep watch for rat droppings, which are like problems. Keep a watch on your accounts, your credit card balances, and your income. As soon as you see rising debts or missed payments, take action.

Don't wait to see the rats, like foreclosure notices and collection agency calls. Rectify the problems ASAP, before they become too big to handle comfortably.

TURN IT AROUND

I saw John, my neighbor, raking leaves. The golden leaves had made a carpet on his front lawn. I walked over to him and said, "This looks so beautiful."

John stopped raking the leaves and looked at me, upset, and said, "You call this beautiful?" (By the way, John is one of the most gentle and soft-spoken people I have known in my life.) After a few moments of silence he said, "You call this shit beautiful and I know why. It's because you have a gardener who does this work for you. This is not beautiful, this is damn ugly!"

I guess he was right. I had it backwards.

Many years later, a snowstorm dumped a foot of snow in my driveway. I said, "Look at this damn mess." I recalled my conversation with John.

I decided to turn it around.

For the next five hours, I shoveled that snow. I kept singing songs aloud: "Thank you, God, for giving this couch potato a chance to refurbish his heart and his muscles. Thank you, God, for giving me the chance to exercise without paying any money to a gym. Thank you, God, for giving me muscles and joints and an ability to shovel. When I am 89 years old, I will look back and be proud that I was able to shovel all this snow at 58 years of age."

Repeatedly and loudly saying these positive statements kept me smiling throughout the day. By the time I finished, it was 5:00 p.m. I stepped into the house still singing. My son stood there watching me through the window. He asked, "Dad! How can you smile and sing after many hours of shoveling?"

I said, "I have a secret."

It is not the problem that is a problem. It is the way you react to the problem that makes it a problem! I saw an opportunity to exercise in cleaning up the snow, so I did not resent it.

STONES IN YOUR PATH

Remove stones lying in your path, otherwise you may stub your toes one of these days.

Resolve problems as they come to you, otherwise they will be in your way when you least desire.

THINK OF DIFFERENT SOLUTIONS

One day I got a shovel and tried to make a flowerbed to plant roses. The ground was so hard that I failed. I asked the lawn man to do it. When I came home in the evening, the flowers were all there in the flowerbeds.

How could he have done it so fast when I was having such trouble?

He had brought twenty bags of top soil, made a four-inch high pile of it, and placed all the plants in them. That is it. He had not dug the soil. He knew it would take a long time to dig the encrusted dirt, so he added soft, nourishing dirt and planted the roses.

Smart, isn't it!

Psychoanalysts used to dig up the past to find solutions in the present. It was expensive and time-consuming. The patients had to come five days a week for hourly sessions, sometimes for five years or more.

Now if someone has problems, CBT therapists do not go into the past. The therapist recognizes the problematic behavior and teaches alternative new skills. New skills bring positive rewards and encourage the patient to keep doing the right thing.

Don't waste your time finding the reasons for your faulty behavior if they are not obvious. Move on to positive behaviors and change your life.

WORRYING

Some people repeat problems in their mind. If they were to type it or write it as they speak to themselves, they would find the same sentences and paragraphs multiple times on a single page.

Think of another person who does not repeat the same problems. Instead, he notes the problem in a clear-cut, crisp sentence. Then he writes possible solutions to the problem and chooses what he feels is the best solution. This person is a problem-solver.

If you start problem-solving in this way, your worries will disappear because you will know that, no matter the problem, you will find an appropriate solution.

DO YOU HAVE A HEADACHE?

You must do everything in your power to get rid of a headache. You wouldn't hit your head with a hammer to get rid of it, right? This would just make your headache that much worse.

Are you stressed out because you have too many problems in your life? Well, do everything in your power to solve them. If you turn to alcohol or drugs to escape your problems, it has the same effect as trying to get rid of a headache by hitting yourself in the head with a hammer. Alcohol will ultimately reduce your sharpness of mind and will interfere with your personal and interpersonal relationships. People will come to know that you are becoming a problem drinker long before you know it yourself.

So don't hit your head with a hammer to get rid of a headache. Look for ways to *solve* the problems, not escape them.

HERD VS. LONE ZEBRA

A lion cannot focus on one zebra to kill if he runs after a herd. As soon as he focuses on one zebra, another one with similar stripes appears in front of his eyes. When he tries to focus on the second one, the third one distracts him. However, if the lion sees a lone zebra, it hunts it down fast because it can focus on the zebra well.

Jack came to me overwhelmed, anxious, and shaking with tension. He was to move overseas within a month.

He had a list of over 100 tasks to do at his old company, his new company, and his house. When he tried to do a task, another task would catch his attention. When he tried to do the second task, a third task would distract him. He got so distracted and anxious that he was having a nervous breakdown.

I asked him to check mark the 20 most important tasks. He quickly did that. Then I asked him to find ten tasks that were more important out of that list of twenty. He did that. Then I asked him to arrange the tasks according to their gravity of consequences. He was able to do that. I asked him to write numbers 1 to 10.

I asked him which one of those tasks he wanted to do in the next two hours. He was to do the rest of the first ten tasks before going to bed.

He decided to postpone multiple tasks for a month like selling the car and cancelling various memberships. I asked him to put the list of postponed tasks away and open it when he went on his first vacation. He suddenly relaxed and I saw a glimmer in his eyes.

He was the lion running after a herd of zebra. Now he is a lion running after a lone zebra, ready for the kill.

DEFEAT THE ENEMY

When you want to defeat an enemy, attack him from the front *and* from behind. When trying to battle the enemy of obesity, stop the food supply route to attack your weight from behind.

You attack the problem from two sides when you want to lose weight. You attack it from the front by exercising and losing calories. Attack it from behind by cutting down on the food supply and calories. You will surely win the battle.

If you are fighting an army and you keep on only attacking the front, the war can go on for a very long time. If you keep on exercising and exercising, you lose little weight. If you adjust the food supply, aka the enemy, you lose weight more rapidly.

THE SNOW STORM

I was anxiously driving to my office, worrying about the forecast of a snowstorm of three to six inches of snow. I worried about a bad drive back home and shoveling snow from my driveway.

I was listening to the news. John Monotone was reporting on the life in New York.

He said, "And here comes a woman dressed in a mink coat. . . . How are you feeling today, Miss?"

She said, "Fine."

He asked, "What is your name?"

She answered, "Lena."

He asked, "Lena, how do you feel about a snowstorm coming today?"

She said, "Fine."

He asked, "Do you feel fine about the 6 inches of snow?"

She answered, "Yes."

He asked, "Where are you from, Lena?"

She replied, "Russia. We have 6 feet of snow. 6 inches of snow is a flurry."

If Lena considered 6 inches of snow as a flurry because she has seen 6 feet of snow, so could I.

Your life is devoid of big health problems, financial disaster, job loss, and family crises. Let's say this is like 5 feet of snow.

Don't worry about the 6 inches of snow. That is someone getting mad at you, or someone getting hurt by what you said. The sunshine melted that snow in my driveway. A long hug and a kiss melted my wife's bad mood away.

Next time when you worry, consider whether you're worrying about a snowstorm or a little flurry.

THE PLAYING CARDS

If you try to make one card stand on its edge, it falls repeatedly. When you place two playing cards with their heads together, they can stand on their edges without falling, leaning on each other for support.

When we put our hands together, we can pick up and lift things we could not have lifted with one hand.

The same is true about solving life's day-to-day problems. When we put our heads together, we can sort out our life's problems better.

Next time, don't hesitate to ask for help.

A PEBBLE AND A BOULDER

A boulder lying in your path is an external problem, which is easily visible. You know where it is and how big it is. You are able to figure out whether to go around it, over it, under it, or to blow it up with dynamite.

A pebble in your shoe is not visible. You do not consider it important enough to get rid of it. You struggle to dismiss this irritation. You would be more comfortable if you got rid of it!

The big problems in your life are obvious. The loss of a job is very stressful, but you know how to look for a new job.

The small pebbles in your psyche are less obvious. Feelings of jealousy, inadequacy, guilt, or inferiority can stay unnoticed even though they keep bothering you throughout the journey of your life. You rarely pause to get rid of them.

Do this by talking to your friends or a therapist.

Either way, once you get rid of the pebbles in your shoe, your life will be more comfortable for you and for those around you.

WAIT FOR THE SUNSHINE

You wanted to put your wash on the line outside to dry, but it was raining. You kept the wet clothes in the house, waited for the sunshine, and only then put the clothes out to dry.

You have a difference of opinion with your loved ones. You are fuming inside. You want to rectify the misunderstanding immediately. You say what's on your mind. The other person is also angry, hurt, and upset. He is not receptive and yells back at you. You feel even more hurt and upset.

Well, that is what I mean by waiting for the sunshine.

Don't put the wet clothes on the line in the rain and expect them to dry. You both need to calm down. Take time off from the problem. Leave it alone for a while. Once both of you are in a better mood, come back again to discuss the issues. There are more chances now that both of you will be open to a truce, a compromise.

THE THIS-OR-THAT TRAP

In concentration camps, guards were posted in the front and the back. The prisoners made a tunnel to the side instead and escaped.

Crises paralyze our problem-solving ability. We start thinking in black and white. It is important at the time to recognize this kind of thinking.

The wise think otherwise.

Take a pencil and paper. Drink some green tea. Write down all courses of action that are humanly possible. Consider every one of them. Choose the best solution.

You will see the escape tunnel at the side of the problem instead of limiting your solutions to front or back exits. You might surprise yourself.

THE DARK NIGHT

A child wakes up in the middle of the night. The fear of darkness grips him. He is afraid that the boogieman will get him. The darker the night is, the more afraid he is that it will never end.

As we age, we realize that the intensity of the darkness does not determine the length of the night.

We have days of financial, interpersonal, emotional, and professional difficulty. The difficulty may be sudden and severe. The crisis becomes the night and the fear of failing becomes the boogieman. We think it is permanent and we become hopeless. We think about ending our life. We forget that every night ends in a day.

Problems always end. Just hang in there until the dark night is over.

GET A NEW KEY

You are trying to open a lock with a key. You have been at it for the last half an hour. You have two choices. Spend another hour using the same key or get a locksmith to make a new one for you.

What would you do?

Tom is a married man. He works very hard. They are having financial problems. He starts a second job. After a while, he feels that maybe he should take a weekend job, too. All along, his relationship with his wife is suffering.

If he continues to use the same strategy, which has not worked, he is destined to fail.

He should consult an accountant or a therapist to find out what is wrong with their money management habits.

Doing more of what does not work will not bring new results. If the old key does not work, make a new key that does.

LIFE'S FLAT TIRES

If you have a flat tire, you do not cancel the journey. You change the tire and move on.

This is true with new problems in life, too. Keep working; solve the problems and move on.

THE HURRICANE WATCH

There was a time when hurricanes created havoc in our lives. We had no time to take cover. Since we developed systems to watch hurricanes, we get a forewarning that a hurricane is in formation. We watch its progression. We take steps to protect ourselves and our homes like boarding glass windows, going to higher ground, or leaving town. Millions of lives have been saved by the fact that we can now watch hurricanes.

Life also has hurricanes; I mean the crises of life. They are unemployment, financial difficulties, separation, and death. Do not get caught in them unprepared. Look out for them. Watch their progression. Make them as predictable as you can. Watch your health by having annual physical examinations. Go to your accountant and look at your financial health. Keep a watch on your loved ones and what is happening to them. Board your life's house.

What do I mean by boarding the house?

I mean making sure that you have adequate life insurance, do preventive car maintenance, and have adequate retirement savings. Assist your loved ones and seek help for their problems.

Those who watch the hurricanes go into their shelters and save themselves. They are prepared.

THE BROKEN TAILLIGHT

I saw that the rear light of my neighbor's car was malfunctioning. After watching it for a week, I pointed it out to him. He thanked me. He said that he was unaware of it. He got it repaired by the next day.

We have many rear lights in our behavior, attitude, personality, and knowledge. We live our lives unaware of them while everyone else notices them. People do not tell us because they believe that we must know such an obvious thing.

Sometimes being aware of our own ignorance helps us. Listening to family and friends helps. They can point out problems you cannot see yourself.

Take a chance to look at your personality to see if it needs repair, like the taillight of a car.

CROSS THE ROAD WITH A PLAN

Generally, you cross the road at an intersection light. You wait for the light to turn to red. You look at the pedestrian walk sign. You then walk with confidence, knowing that the traffic has stopped and will not start until you have crossed the road.

Sometimes, you have to cross the road when the crossing is far away from you. When you take a step to cross the road, traffic comes from the right. When you try again, it comes from the left. It makes you very anxious. In a situation like this, you decide to walk to the middle of the road, when the half of the road next to you is clear. Once you are in the middle of the road on the yellow line, you cross the next half when the next break comes.

Tom was hospitalized and endured an extended healing period. By the time he rejoined his job as an investment advisor in his bank, all his customers had moved on. His referral tree had dried up. If he waited for his business to develop, the bank would foreclose his house. He had used up his life's savings during the sick period.

We discussed a strategy. Both of his concerns were justified. He had to make money for paying his rent now and keeping his job at the old bank as an investment advisor was important.

I suggested to him that he decide to cross the road in two steps. He takes a job as a waiter in the evening. Let the money come in to take care of the essentials. He then will have to stand there in the middle of the road of life and wait for the traffic to clear and cross the second half. He started working in the evening as a waiter. He kept his mornings for his bank clients. It took a long time to revive his business in the bank, but he did it.

He had crossed the busy road of life in spite of the oncoming traffic of financial difficulty from one side and loss of his dream from the other side.

EMOTIONAL TICK

When you return from a walk in the woods, doctors recommend examining exposed areas of your body to locate a blood-sucking tick.

Diane met Jack at a dance. He was cute, so Diane gave him her phone number. He has been calling her ever since. He is causing unhappiness. If she does not return his phone call soon, he becomes offended. When she talks about her day, he finds faults with her. She is wondering about her relationship with him. "He *was* cute," she thinks. She has been unable to focus on her work because of all the distractions.

She picked up Jack, who is like a tick, from the club, which is like the woods. Jack has latched on to her and is very demanding of her time. The faster she gets rid of him, the safer she is. The longer she hesitates pulling Jack away from her life, the weaker she is going to get.

Search your life well. If you find an emotional tick stuck to you, pull it out and get rid of it.

DID YOU STUB YOUR TOE?

While walking barefoot in your home, you stub your toe on a piece of furniture. You cry and rub the toe for relief. You stub your toe again on the same piece of furniture later. That is excruciatingly painful.

When your toe gets stubbed one time, I would call it bad luck. You stub your toe twice because you did not wear a shoe, rearrange your furniture, or pay more attention to where you were walking.

Carelessness is inaction to prevent mistakes. Do not blame your luck.

MIDDLE GROUND

A room with clutter looks messy. This is true. Add one more thing to that chaos and you cannot notice the change. However, take a room with everything in its proper place. Now throw a pen or a shoe on the carpet; it shouts at you.

Jan met Steve in college. He is a great person but she was shocked to see chaos in his room. He had piled his shoes, clothes, books, and shirts in one corner. He was talking about his recent football game with such passion that everything else seemed unimportant.

Now they live in a house. The house looks very neat and clean. Jan hates the sight of his desk and repeatedly reminds him to take care of it. He tells her that he is in the middle of his work and that the books and journals are open at certain pages on purpose. In that spic and span house, the messy desk makes Jan go crazy. She calls him a pig. He calls her a nagging obsessive person.

Our life may be chaotic or overly organized. Both of the lifestyles can create distress. What is important is to keep things in moderation. The house does not have to look spic and span like Jan's room, nor should it look like Steve's dorm room.

If they live together, they will have to accept a middle ground in cleanliness and clutter.

LEARN TO RECOGNIZE MULTIPLE CHOICES

When you take a test, you have to find the right answer out of four options: A, B, C, and D. You think and select the most appropriate one.

Every decision in life has multiple choices, out of which you have to make the right selection. By habit, you select from one or two choices that come to mind. You make yourself miserable if both are unacceptable to you.

There are always more choices available. Search for them and then decide.

AVOID THE PUDDLES

Do you remember a time when it was raining and snowing? It made puddles and slippery spots outside. You went outside and walked only on the dry spots. You did not step in any puddles.

There are times in our lives when problems pour down like rain.

There are puddles of problems. We find small islands of strength as we go through the difficult times. Eventually, our relationships, problems at work, and finances normalize.

When there are puddles in your life, remember that there are dry spots of friends and hobbies in between. Keep moving.

BRICKS ON A MUDDY PATH

The rain made the path next to our house muddy. A neighbor put bricks down in such a way that I could walk on them and avoid soiling my shoes on rainy days.

Jack lost his job due to downsizing at his company. There was no money and life came to a standstill.

Jack took action by laying the bricks of free computer lessons at the employment office, mowing lawns in his neighborhood, reducing their expenses, taking the kids out of day care, and being the house dad.

These steps were like those bricks on the muddy path that helped him to deal with the financial crisis.

REDUCE STRESS

Little things can cause stress.

You want a can of soda. The vending machine at work accepts change but you have dollar bills. You keep change at home but you do not bring it. You leave the keys to the office at home. You find out that you left your eyeglasses at home. A cop stops you; you do not have your license because you left your wallet at home. You discover at a crucial time that your cell phone has run out of charge. Let us suppose that each one of these things happens once per day. You can be sure that you will accumulate stress.

Before I leave my house, I spend less than ten seconds every day and look at a checklist. This habit has spared me from countless stressful moments over the years.

Try making checklists. They work.

COMPLEX PROBLEMS AND SIMPLE SOLUTIONS

Frequent seizures resulted in several hospitalizations for my patient. Each hospitalization was expensive. I kept asking, "Why is this patient's epilepsy not stabilizing?" In time, I found out that the patient missed his noon dose because he was busy at work, even though the pills were right in his pocket.

Together we came up with the idea of a wristwatch with an alarm set for 8:00 a.m., noon, and 8:00 p.m. With this solution, the patient's epilepsy was under control.

The most complex problem can have a very simple solution. Look for it.

Now take it one step further. Sometimes we know the solution, but remain stuck in our familiar pattern. Perhaps you are always late for work, yet you continue to oversleep and live with the stress of being late. Once you know the solution, act on it.

Find a simple solution. Give a quarter to your secretary if you are late. You will be amazed that a simple trick like that will help you be on time.

BE LIKE A TEA KETTLE

Steam had collected in a boiler because no one had checked the pressure gauge. The boiler exploded. Two men lost their lives.

The steam boiler needs someone to monitor its pressure gauge. The pressure must be released when it is dangerously high.

Have you ever heard of a teakettle exploding? It does not collect steam; it releases it. The kettle makes a lot of whistling noise to let everyone know that it wants to get off the hot burner.

When you begin to develop inner anger or discomfort, act like the tea kettle. "Whistle" to let others know that you need help. They will come to your rescue. If you keep collecting steam, you will explode in an angry outburst. People will run away from you.

People will respond to a whistle, a request for help; they will rush to help you let off some steam.

DO NOT CUT FROZEN BUTTER

A frozen bar of butter is as hard as a stone. If you try cutting one, it will slip and fall on the floor. If you hold it tightly, your knife may slip and injure your hand. Leave it for a few minutes to thaw. Once it is softer, you will have no problem slicing through it.

Occasionally your spouse, friend, parent, or boss is adamant in his opinion. You try hard to change his opinion but he remains adamant. If you pound him with arguments and counter arguments, he will withdraw or retaliate against you.

So do not try to cut a frozen bar of butter!

Leave that frozen person alone. Ask him to take his time and think about it. Let the time pass. Thaw him with the warmth of your company, love, affection, and friendship. When you feel that he has softened and is in a good mood, come back with your request. Chances are much better that he will accept it.

WHO DOESN'T?

Psychiatrists, psychologists, marriage counselors, therapists, physicians, clergy, as well as great leaders have had relationship problems. As long as you have relationships, you will have problems.

Relationship problems are universal.

Having problems is not your failure. It is a failure if you don't address the problems and try to solve them. Start working to find solutions. The more you focus on solving the problems, the more successful you will be in your relationships.

CAN ONE STRANDED MOTORIST HELP ANOTHER?

You are traveling on a highway. Suddenly you have a flat tire. You do not have a spare tire or a cell phone.

You see another disabled car half a mile away. What can a disabled car driver do to help another disabled car driver? Yet you walk over and talk. He has been standing there for the last hour because he ran out of gas. You talk to each other. You decide to give him some of your gasoline and he loans you his spare tire. Both of you resume your journey.

All of us have problems. Our family members, friends, and colleagues have problems. Talking about our problems with family, friends, or a professional can give us new insight into its solution. Do not make the mistake of saying to yourself, "How can she help me, she can't even help herself."

You just never know who can help you until you try.

PUT SENSE INTO YOUR OWN HEAD

Do you surprise yourself when you solve your friend's problems with ease? Your friend looks at you with appreciation and gratitude. He thanks you for your wise counsel. On the other hand, you find yourself angry, upset, and helpless when things happen in your own life. You get those crazy ideas and crazy emotions which paralyze you. You wonder why you cannot resolve your own problems.

Your confused self, full of fears, is the emotional self you brought with you from your childhood. That is the little child in you who is impulsive, demanding, and wants things *now* at any cost. It pulls you down.

The part of you that helps your friends is your mature self. You acquired it through emotional maturity later in life. Use your ability to solve problems for yourself. This is your hidden resource.

Talk to the child inside you loudly and tell him why you think he is right or wrong. You can use a tape recorder and listen to your own suggestions. I bet you will be thanking yourself for your wise counsel.

PROBLEMS

Problems are a part of our lives. The more successful we are, the more problems we have.

If we have a job, we have work problems.

If we have a spouse, we have relationship problems.

If we have a car, we have car expenses.

If we have children, they will have their problems.

The only people who do not have any problems are the people in the cemetery. They do not worry about bills, car troubles, or a mortgage.

They do not have problems, but they also lack the joy of living.

Next time you have problems, remember to thank God for your life instead of dwelling on an issue. Every problem has a solution. Most problems have more than one solution. It's up to you to find it.

FINANCIAL HARDSHIPS

My father used to say that the essential things in life are free. The unessential things are most expensive. He would say that the most essential thing you need to stay alive is air and water. Air is free. Water is almost free. The third basic requirement is food. Luckily, most of us can afford simple food. The fourth necessity is shelter. That is expensive. The cost increases as you add on nonessential items: a bigger house, expensive food, drinks, and fine furnishings.

The most expensive things are unnecessary for life: travel, entertainment, jewelry, restaurants, glamorous clothing, and automobiles.

This concept helps us to keep our priorities straight and avoid panic during financial hard times.

SURVIVING THE STORM

While experiencing a storm, the only thing you must do is survive. Do the most essential things to keep you alive. Hold on to something solid and lay low in a corner of the basement. When the storm is gone, come out to find out what the damage is and how to take care of it.

At times, your relationships and life circumstances will throw you into an emotional storm. You will not be able to analyze, be objective, or deal with problems rationally. You must try to *survive*. The storm may be unemployment, severe illness, injury, loss of a relationship, or death of a loved one. Just do the essential things, like a robot. Take care of your water intake, eat three meals a day, dress yourself, and keep working so that money keeps coming in. Eventually, the crisis will be over and then you can slowly pick up the pieces.

Remember, just as the storm does not stay forever, the crisis in your life will not last forever. Each crisis will eventually subside, allowing you to brace yourself for the next one.

BALL AND TRAMPOLINE

Every time the ball fell on the trampoline it bounced, causing stress to the trampoline. The trampoline begged the ball not to bounce on it. It requested the ball to shrink in size, but the ball would not listen. It remained unchanged, and each fall on the trampoline caused the trampoline the stress of stretching.

One day the trampoline heard the serenity prayer: "God, grant me the serenity to accept the things I cannot change, the courage to change the things I can, and the wisdom to know the difference."

It realized that it had no control over the weight of the ball. The trampoline could ask and beg, but the ball would not change its size. The trampoline realized that it *could* change itself. Bingo! The trampoline lessened its tension. It became more relaxed from that day onwards.

The same ball, with the same weight, fell on the trampoline again but this time just sank into the lap of the relaxed trampoline. It could not bounce as it did before. The ball's wicked smirk was replaced with surprise. Again, it tried to create a big bounce, but the same thing happened. The ball just sank there.

By changing itself, the trampoline had solved its problem with the ball.

ARE YOU A FISH OR A WATER LILY?

A fish lives in a pond, sometimes in clean water and sometimes in dirty water. The water lily in the same pond rises above the water. The water lily has the pond water below it, but its blossoms float above it. Dirty or clean water does not affect it.

When people around you are arguing and you become a part of it, you are like the fish in the pond. You are yelling, screaming, and adding to the chaos, to the dirt in the water. Try to be the water lily. Distance yourself from the arguments. Listen to everyone's point of view. Do not ask whose fault it is. Instead, ask what the problem is and what you can do to help solve it.

Stop getting defensive and stop attacking others. Ask yourself, what is the problem? What can I do to help resolve it? Work towards becoming the water lily and get yourself out of the murky pond of arguments.

MORE SOLUTIONS CAN BE FOUND

Suppose you are out for a hike and you come across a huge boulder in your path. Your immediate reaction is to think about what you must do next. If you can't think of how to get around it, do you sit down and give up?

In life when you come across a difficult boulder of a problem, the usual response is, "I cannot do this." We had one solution that is not possible so we give up. Take a step back and think of all the alternate solutions that are possible. If you cannot think of the solution, ask a friend, a colleague, a guide, a teacher, or your spouse. When you are explaining the problem aloud, alternate solutions may come to you.

You could climb over it, tunnel under it, go back home and maybe return when you have more time, destroy it and sell the pieces, go around it, or decide that this journey isn't worth the trouble. Regardless of which you choose, there are always many solutions to a problem if you just take a moment to *really* look.

HABIT REPLACEMENT

A snake grows new skin. The old skin lifts off of its body and the snake crawls out of it.

The same applies to us human beings. We feel helpless in getting rid of our old habits even though we know that they do not serve us anymore.

Develop new habits instead of fighting old habits. Let us suppose that every night you open several cans of beer while watching TV. You soon recognize that it is becoming a bad habit but continue every night.

During that time, go to the gym and work out.

Before you know it, you will have grown a new habit of going to the gym and crawled out of your sedentary TV watching and beer drinking habit.

Beating Negative Thinking

"WHAT IF" CAN BE BAD OR GOOD

We frighten ourselves with "what if" thoughts. What if an accident happens? What if I lose my job? What if the world is submerged in water and we all die?

We scare ourselves. Statistically the chances of bad and good events are random. Let us turn the tide around.

Start replacing fearful what ifs with encouraging ones.

What if my day is beautiful?

What if I succeed in my business?

What if I live a long and healthy life?

What if I do my job well?

What if I am a safe driver?

What if the world continues for another million or billion years?

Until now you have scared yourself with bad what ifs; now make yourself happy with good what ifs.

STEERING YOUR EMOTIONS

When you drive your car, you are the driver. You use the steering wheel to control your wheels to change the direction of the car and hence your destination.

Let's apply this idea to thoughts.

You are the driver in your brain. You decide what emotions you want to experience; that is your destination. You use the steering wheel of your mind, i.e. your thoughts, to control your emotions, the wheels of your mind's car.

If you notice that your car is going to a dirt road exit you do not intend to travel down, you immediately turn your steering wheel. That changes the direction of your wheels. That in turn changes the direction of your car and you come back to the main highway.

Therefore, when you note that you are going into a sad mood, the dirt road, you immediately turn your steering wheel (your thoughts). You practice positive self-talk. That in turn changes the direction of your wheels (your emotions).

Emotions reside somewhere in your mind and body. They seem out of reach. By recognizing that your thoughts are in your full control, you become the master of your emotions.

ONCE YOU COULDN'T; NOW YOU CAN

As I relate the following story, I apologize for my behavior during childhood. We were six years old. We thought this was a fine way to spend time.

My friends and I would catch a duck from a pond and force it to lie on its back with its feet facing us. The duck struggled to get away at first but we held it still for a few minutes. Finally, the duck would give up and stop struggling. Slowly we would remove our hands and back away from the duck. The duck would not get up and waddle away. It would lie there for many minutes without moving. It did not realize that the forces holding it down were gone. Sometimes we had to turn the duck upright before it would return to the pond.

Similarly, when we fail to achieve, we give up. As time and circumstances change, we become capable of achieving those things, but like the duck, we do not realize our opportunity and do not attempt again to achieve them.

Think of a little girl who tries to befriend a boy with whom she has fallen in love. The little boy shows more interest in his friends than in the little girl. Her heart is broken. She grows up believing that she is not attractive and she will be rejected again.

She is unaware that time has changed. She has grown into a lovable young woman and the little boy is now interested in her. If she were to open herself to the idea that time has changed, she would find the same boy interested in her.

In the past, she could not: now she can.

Think what you failed in and gave up in the past. Revise your evaluation of yourself and your worth. Find out what you could not do back then and what you can do now.

DELETE YOUR JUNK MAIL

You get all kinds of emails. Some are joyful, informative, and essential; others are obscene, hostile, and contain a virus. If you are naïve, you open all of them. The opened virus emails infect and disable your computer. If you are computer savvy, you don't open them. You simply delete them.

Our mind is like our email inbox, too. It gets all kinds of thoughts. Some are problems, solutions, or joyful; others are nasty, evil, and unwanted. If you attend to these evil thoughts, you become unhappy, scared, and guilty, and wonder what kind of an evil person you are.

Think of these thoughts the way you think of spam. Do not open them; just delete them. The important thing is what you do with your thoughts. You have no control over *getting* those thoughts in your mind. The only thing you have control of is how much attention and time you spend on them.

ANTIDOTE THOUGHTS

If someone overdoses on heroin, they can often be revived with a Narcan injection as an antidote.

Every time Joe went away for a business trip, Rita, his wife, would go crazy. She worried about an air disaster by a terrorist bomb. She could not eat or sleep while he was away. She knew her worries were irrational but she could not control her thoughts. She asked Joe to change jobs.

Poisonous thoughts also have antidote thoughts.

Rita decided to use antidote thoughts for her fears. She repeatedly told herself, "He has one in 5,000 chances of dying in his car on the highway. He has one in 11 million chances of dying in an air disaster. Why am I worrying when he is so much safer in the air?"

By repeatedly giving herself antidote thoughts, she was able to calm her anxiety and it eventually went away.

OPEN THE WINDOWS

Anna was injured on the job. She was on permanent disability from her job for years. She stayed in her home alone. She could not drive to go places. She became lonely and depressed. A sense of hopelessness, uselessness, and helplessness started descending on her. The normal behavior of her husband started bothering her. She tried her best but could not dispel the dark shadows of sadness.

Open the windows and the darkness goes away.

I encouraged her to make phone calls to family and friends and go to church. She was hesitant to call others for help. She was ashamed. I asked her how she felt when others asked her to help them. She said that she felt very good helping others. I told her that when she asks for help, she would make others feel good, too.

She started socializing, going out, and calling friends and neighbors. She was amazed to find that people enjoyed listening to her and helping her. She was very good with computers. She started helping other people sell their stuff on eBay. The windows of her relationships with people started lifting the darkness of depression.

When you have shadows of depression, open the windows to relationships and activities.

YOUR HEART BELIEVES YOUR THOUGHTS

When you tell a child that the boogeyman is coming, he gets scared and starts crying. You, as an adult, know that the boogeyman is not real. A child does not have maturity to differentiate. Therefore, if you do not want the child to cry for the next hour, do not scare him by saying that the boogeyman is coming.

Your brain is only capable of analyzing what is real and not real. Your heart, like a child, believes what your brain tells it. If you say in your mind, "no one cares," your heart will respond with sadness. Your heart obeys your careless thoughts. Be very careful about what you think.

If a child is crying, you can ask what scared him. He will tell you.

Whenever you see an emotion in your heart like sadness, ask yourself what your brain was telling your heart. Those confusing emotions will become easy to understand and take care of.

Don't scare yourself by saying scary things in your mind.

GET OUT OF YOUR OWN WAY

Did someone stand in your way and stop you from doing what you wanted to do?

Was it your dad?

Was it you mom?

Who is stopping you now? That person who holds you back could be you.

Have you ever felt that you have stood in *your own* path? Have you ever noticed that you discourage yourself from doing anything positive? You blame yourself for taking an action and you frighten yourself with thoughts of failure or fear.

Get out of your own way and move on with your life!

WHAT ARE YOU STORING IN YOUR HEAD?

If you keep on collecting garbage in your home, you will have a stinky house. However, if you collect flowers and open the windows, you are going to have a nice, fresh fragrance in your home.

If you keep on thinking unhappy thoughts about past mistakes, anger, injustice, fear, and bad luck, you will become depressed. These thoughts will make your mental and emotional life stink.

On the other hand, you could open the windows of your mind and let these negative thoughts out. Also, bring new blossoms of good thoughts: friends, hobbies, music, and fun activities. Your inner mind is going to smell like a bouquet of flowers.

Next time if your life stinks, ask yourself what you are storing in your head. Is it garbage? Or is it flowers?

KILL NEGATIVE THOUGHTS

What happens when you see a fly in the room? The buzzing of the fly is annoying. It distracts you from whatever you are doing. You get up, take a fly swatter, and kill it. Good! That is what you should do, and do it ASAP.

Upsetting thoughts about past mistakes, hurts, and transgressions are like flies. They can enter in the room of your present life through a window of time. The thoughts buzz through your mind. They distract you from your tasks. They produce shame, guilt, and sadness. They annoy and depress you.

So watch out! If you find a negative thought from your past haunting your present, treat it like a fly. Kill it. It has no place in your present.

DON'T LET THE EGGS HATCH

Do not make yourself miserable if you have strange thoughts. Simply delete them.

If you had a scorpion's eggs, you would want to make sure that they don't hatch. If they hatch, you will end up with live baby scorpions. The more eggs you have, the more scorpions will sting you.

Self-depreciating thoughts are like the scorpion's harmless eggs. If you do not voice them, they will lie dormant in your mind and then die off.

Voicing of your thoughts is like hatching them. If you hatch a criticism by stating it out loud, it will bring negative consequences. Bitter words have the sting of a scorpion.

The spoken words travel through your voice and into your ears. Once in your brain, they produce more "eggs" of thoughts and actions. Your brain will become a thought hatchery. This creates a vicious cycle of criticisms and negative self-talk.

Bite your tongue. Keep your criticism in your mind. If you hatch the "eggs" by speaking, your words will hurt you or others, like baby scorpions.

DON'T LET THE BURS TANGLE

Do you remember going through the woods? When you came out, you saw there were prickly little burs stuck to your clothes. You pulled them off with some effort and walked away. If you left them too long, they were tangled and destroyed your clothing.

Negative thoughts, which stick to your mind while you walk through life, are like burs. Please watch for them, catch them, pull them off, and throw them away. If you don't do this repeatedly, the bad thoughts will remain stuck to your mind, become tangled, and cause discontent.

DON'T LET YOUR ENGINE IDLE

If your car idles, it heats up the engine and exhausts gasoline. You find your gas tank empty while you're on your journey or an overheated engine stalls your car.

Worry is like the idling of the mind's engine. It exhausts your emotional, psychic, and spiritual energy.

When it comes to living and doing real life work, you find that you are tired and unmotivated.

Switch off your mental engine when you detect worry about trivial things.

PEST PROBLEMS

Our negative thoughts are like rats. Once they come into our mind, they produce rat droppings of anxiety, depression, jealousy, guilt, frustration, and anguish. The rats of thoughts nibble and destroy our self-confidence and self-image. If left unattended, the negative thoughts reproduce. If left unchecked, they can plague our mind.

When you notice the rat droppings of negative emotions, watch out for hidden rats of thoughts.

Watch the rats of thoughts like a hawk. When you see rats of negative thoughts, swoop down and kill them before they destroy your peace.

Keep your mind free of those rat-thoughts. You will remain free of the droppings of negative emotions.

DON'T BASE LOVE ON FEAR

Wanting to have a partner is natural, but a belief that you cannot survive without one makes you anxious. You will look for a marriage partner in panic. Once you are married, you will be fearful of separation, divorce, or death. The marriage is like an emotional boat in the sea of life. It gives you security.

Nevertheless, you should be able to swim if the boat capsizes.

Live your married life in a way that you can survive if you lose your partner. Only then will you truly enjoy the marriage instead of living in fear.

THE LIGHT OF KNOWLEDGE

When I was five years old, I had a fear of demons hiding in the darkness under my bed. I used to jump from my bed to my chair so they would not bite my legs off. At some point during those years, I looked under the bed with a flashlight. I did not see any demons.

Sometimes we get lost in the darkness of our fears. We are afraid that if we have a pap smear, we will find cervical cancer; hence, we avoid having the test performed. Some women avoid mammograms for fear that they might find out they have breast cancer. Postponing turning the lights on only prolongs and perpetuates our fears.

Remember: as long as I did not look under the bed with a flashlight, I believed there were demons there.

The light of knowledge will dispel the fears of ignorance.

INSECURITY HIJACKING

Amy was driving through a tunnel that goes under the Hudson River. It is a long tunnel. As Amy's car entered the tunnel, a thought crossed her mind: "What if the walls crack and the river rushes into the tunnel?" She visualized the water rushing in. She saw herself gasping for air and drowning. She saw her children sobbing over her body. She saw her husband marrying Angela, their neighbor. Her head and heart were pounding. Her hands became sweaty. Her knuckles turned white as she clenched the steering wheel.

In reality, nothing happened. The tunnel has existed since 1927 and 34 million cars pass through it every year. The tunnel is going to serve many decades safely.

Your thoughts of jealousy, fear, insecurity, and guilt may suddenly pop up and drown you. Keep a close watch on them. Ask yourself, "Is this a reality or a fantasy? How likely is it that this will actually happen? Is it possible that *nothing* bad will happen?" When you challenge your own thoughts, you will be amazed to see how calm and stable your mind will become.

Don't let your insecurities hijack your thoughts.

DO WHAT MAKES YOU HAPPY

Make believe that you are in a dark cave where you cannot see your way out. One day, you see a very small spot of light. Do you ignore the light or proceed towards it? Go towards that spot of light and finally you emerge into the open sunshine.

Sometimes life turns into a dark and dingy cave of problems, rejections, failures, and abandonment. You go from one day to the next with a sinking feeling of despair that you will never find your way out of that cave of despair.

One day you suddenly find slight joy, happiness, or laughter. Perhaps you visited a health club. Do not just let it pass as one good moment. Latch onto it. Become a member of the gym. If walking through the park made you feel better, grab that feeling. Join an area-hiking club. If you enjoyed bowling, join a league. If you enjoy your computer, take an evening class to improve your skills. Actively seek out whatever it is that gives momentary joy.

The idea is to lengthen those blips of happy moments into minutes, hours, and days until you find yourself in the sunshine of life again.

PLAY YOUR THOUGHTS ACTIVELY

A guitar with tightly wound strings will make a slight humming noise. The currents of the air produce vibrations to give that hum. If that hum bothers you, pick up the guitar and play it. Now you will hear your song instead.

When we vegetate, our minds produce thoughts. They can be negative thoughts of past frustrations and failures. It is very important to recognize what kind of thoughts are humming through the guitar of your mind. If these thoughts are bothersome to you, do not let them go on. Decide to think of some positive aspect of your life. Make a conscious effort to think of something that gives you hope, joy, and a sense of achievement.

Do not let your mind wander into a dull hum. Choose the thoughts that you actively play and enjoy the music.

SHORT-LIVED RAINDROP MOMENTS

Have you ever watched the rain through your window? The drops fall into puddles and form bubbles for a split second. The lifespan of a bubble is very short. Every raindrop bubble lived, but in the scheme of life, it has no meaning.

In the scheme of your life, many things will happen to you. Events will occur; friends, brothers, sisters, coworkers or customers will get mad, angry, or upset with you. These situations will occur repeatedly. Each upsetting event is like a raindrop bubble; it has a life of its own. Remember that these events are short-lived.

If you look back at your life, you will see that hundreds of events have happened. You remember just a few. Most of the unpleasant, upsetting events have faded in your memory.

The next time someone gets upset with you, watch it through the window of your life. See this event as a raindrop bubble that is short-lived. It will die and a new raindrop will replace it.

SOOTHING MEMORIES

Whenever your hands need soothing, what do you do? I am sure you would not rub sandpaper on your hands! Instead, you take out the hand cream and gently massage it into your skin.

When you feel low, sad, or hurt, go back in your memory bank and bring out the soothing lotion of good, comforting memories of the positive events in your life. Keep a list of these good times and review them when you need relief.

Do not mull over the unfortunate and painful hurts and losses. During difficult times, the tendency is to bring back all the misfortune that has struck you. They will be to your emotional state like sandpaper is on your hands. They will increase your pain and distress.

Realize that what you think is under *your* control. Use this ability and bring calming relief when you need it.

DON'T BE A COMPLAINER

People spend their energy complaining about weather or other things in their life. They say, "I hate this miserable weather." If the day is nice, they say, "I hate to be working. I would rather play golf."

You can complain but the weather takes its own course.

Some people make themselves experts at finding faults in people, things, their environment, family, restaurants, food, and whatever else they can find. They complain; it does not matter what about. The complainer will say, "I look horrible today."

Complaining is healthy when you rectify a problem with a product you purchased or an error with your bank account.

However, a frequent complainer may create a stink for people around them. So, watch what comes out of your mouth when you open it next time! Do not complain as a habit.

EMOTIONAL CHEWING GUM

You chew a piece of gum until your jaw aches. You neither swallow it nor get any nourishment from it. In contrast, you *eat* an apple. You bite, chew, swallow, and move on.

Worrying is like emotionally chewing gum.

There are thoughts that go around and around in your head. Do not dwell on a worry until you develop a headache and still have no solution. Stop the emotional chewing gum.

To do this, think clearly. Delineate the problem. Consider many possible solutions. Decide on the best solution and act on it, then move on.

DON'T LOOP YOUR THOUGHTS

A regular audio cassette has a beginning and an end.

Sometimes the message on an audio tape plays for a set amount of time and repeats the same statements over and over. When you call a busy organization, they play a loop when you are on hold.

Your thinking can be like an audio cassette. You think of a problem, consider the possible solutions, and choose the best one. We call this problem-solving. It has a beginning and an end.

The second kind of thinking is like an audio loop. It repeats itself:

"Why did my sister say that? I don't like the way she treats me. I get so aggravated. I should have told her off, but she may get offended because she can't take it. *She* can say whatever she wants to, but when I reciprocate, she gets all huffy and puffy. I can't believe she can say things like that. . . ."

This endless loop causes tension, anxiety, depression, and agitation.

So cut the loop as soon as you recognize it. Try problem-solving instead.

QUALITY CONTROL

Products pass through a quality control room before they are shipped for sale. The quality control inspectors discard defective merchandise. Some factories do not manage their quality control room well. Defective merchandise leaves the factory for sale, giving the company a bad name.

Your mind is a thought manufacturing factory. It is manufacturing thoughts, ideas, desires, impulses, and wishes 24 hours a day. Even as you sleep, your brain factory produces thoughts that you see as dreams. Some of them are absurd and unbelievable. Some of them are immoral, blasphemous, or illegal things you would never actually do. They include anger at your loved ones, sexual contacts with forbidden people, or blasphemous thoughts about your higher power. You are scared that you will act them out. They make you feel guilty, unhappy, and fearful.

Remember: the brain is a thought manufacturing factory.

Don't be scared of your bad thoughts. You have a quality control room in your head. It is your judgment. It will stop you from acting out a bad thought, wish, or desire.

Your good judgment will let you carry out good desires and actions while filtering out the bad.

DON'T MAGNIFY YOUR PROBLEMS

Project a large picture of a mosquito on a screen. Project a small picture of a lion on that screen, too. At that moment, the mosquito invokes more fear than the lion.

In stressful situations, we become very critical of ourselves. We start focusing on our small defects, mistakes, and criticism we've heard from others. We enlarge them in our minds. They look incredibly scary to us. In that mindset, we forget that the real problem is relatively small.

It is very important to realize at that time that even though the problem has been enlarged to a 16-foot by 16-foot screen, the real size of this mosquito of a problem is less than half a centimeter and can be killed with bug spray.

Don't enlarge your problems in the heat of the moment.

PULL THE WEEDS

If you are a gardener, you know that a good lawn is the result of pulling out or destroying all the weeds, which grow automatically. They are harmful and aggressive with deep roots and soon tend to overpower the soft, vulnerable grass. If you let them stay there, they flower and throw new seeds. Soon the weeds totally take over and destroy the lawn.

Similarly, maladaptive thoughts, impulses, and ideas can cross your mind, which is counteractive to your happiness in the long run. If you are married, impulses come to cheat on your spouse. If you are a student, impulses are to spend time drinking in a bar instead of studying.

These impulses and desires are like weeds in your mind. It is important to recognize them, pull them out, and throw them away. They will come again, and when they do, you just keep on pulling them out and throwing them away again and again. Getting into this good habit will ensure that your lawn—your thoughts—are beautiful and serve you well.

BEHAVIOR FRIES

You buy a package of French fries. If you cook them and find a few that are overcooked or undercooked, you throw them away and eat the rest.

A blob of mashed potatoes is either good or bad. You eat it all or throw it all away.

Do not use derogatory terms like, "failure," "inferior," or, "loser," as if you were a blob of inedible mashed potatoes.

Treat yourself like a package of French fries. Ask yourself which part of you is a French fry that is good and useful and make the most of what is good about yourself. Ask yourself which behavior of yours is a problem and get rid of it.

Letting Go & Living Now

VISITING VS. LIVING IN THE PAST

"You have no clue how much I suffered in my childhood. Bad things happened there. My mother was controlling and my dad yelled at me for bringing home a B+. He ignored all the A's."

Why is it that even though you are a doctor, you feel like a failure? In addition, even though you are a capable man, you feel controlled by your secretary in your office and by your wife at home. You remain angry. They complain that it is very difficult to please you. You are always irritable and nasty.

It is because you live in the past and see others as your father and mother. You are not able to take pride in your achievements and make independent decisions. You see yourself as a little boy that has become a doctor but has continued to stay in your childhood home.

Grow up!

Your mother is a frail old woman now; your father is a frail old man now. They have no power. They depend on *you* for little favors.

While you live in the present, you can import of the happy memories from your childhood.

Import happy memories but don't live in the negatives you lived in back then.

PHOTO ALBUM OF YOUR LIFE

You keep thinking about the past and become unhappy.

You pick up your childhood photo album and look at the pictures. You look at them repeatedly if they make you happy. You close the album, lock it away, and forget about it.

You are the owner of the album. The album is not your owner.

You can bring past memories into the present. You can then open the album of past memories and enjoy the photos you like. Use your past if it makes you happy.

If it makes you unhappy, keep the past memory album in a lock box. Do not look at it and make yourself miserable. Remember: you are the owner of the album. The album is not your owner.

DON'T FEED YOUR DAY TO THE PAST

You have been spending time thinking about the past. You regret how you treated your family, your friends, and opportunities that presented themselves. You regret your bad decisions and wasted time.

You wasted some of your time *in* the past and now you are wasting your today *on* the past.

Whether you waste your time *in* the past or *on* the past, the important lesson is that you are taking your today and feeding it *to* the past.

Stop.

Live today.

LIVING IS YOUR BUSINESS

Nature gave you birth. You have no control of that. Nature will also give you death. You do not have control over that, either… it will surely happen.

Living is your business. Make the best of it.

Many of us worry about what will happen in the future. Will I die young? Will I get sick? These questions take your precious time away from you.

Use your eyes to look at the beautiful trees swaying in the wind. Look at the flowers around you. Look at beautiful buildings. Look at the sky; it's always there for you. Look at your beautiful family.

Use your ears to listen to music or to your friends and family. Call a friend you have not spoken with in a while. Make delicious food. Eat tasty things and enjoy every morsel. Don't be one of those people that finish their lunch without even realizing what they ate.

The next time you start worrying about your death, remind yourself: "My birth and death are God's headache. Let me live and enjoy my life."

ENJOY THE ORANGE SLICE

When you go to a Chinese restaurant, they bring fortune cookies and an orange cut into slices after a meal. You pick up a slice and bite the juicy flesh of the orange, leaving only the peel behind. You taste all that juice and freshness in your mouth.

Each day is like another section of that orange called life. Take the joy out of each day like flesh from the orange slice. Don't try to save it for your retirement days. By that time the orange will rot.

People hold off on travel, fun, golf, and many other activities, saving them for their retirement days. When retirement arrives, arthritis or other afflictions do not allow them to do any of those things.

Enjoy your orange slices today. Don't save them for later; you never know what life will bring you that may hinder your ability to enjoy them later.

PAIN OF THE PAST

Let's imagine that you have a hole in your back yard. You have tried to fill it but it remains empty. Each time you go to the back yard, you fall into it. What do you do?

You decide to work on your front lawn. You spend your time, effort, and money on the grass, flowering plants, patio furniture, statues, and trees in the front lawn. You make it so beautiful that you want to spend more time in it. Now you don't miss your back lawn as frequently. Please note that the hole is still there in the back lawn but it does not make you as sad as it did.

The more time you spend fulfilling your present life, the more the pain of your past will decrease. Spend your energy in making your present livable rather than trying to repair the past losses.

FALLEN IN THE WELL!

You are running for your life, away from a predator. In your frantic confusion, you fall into a well. You are safe in the well. The predator cannot reach you.

So you wait and cautiously come out of the well after a while to see that it is safe now. It is okay to move on with your life under the blue skies.

Alternatively, if you get very scared, you decide to stay in the well forever. You remain alive in the well but have no work, no friends, no play, and no activities. Your life has become focused on survival instead of living.

The same happens to people who are rejected in a relationship, lose a job, or get injured at work. The new lifestyle of social withdrawal and limited activities depresses them. Attention from people, doctors, insurance companies, and regular disability income becomes their life. It is free of risks but it is a shell of a life. It is a colorless sketch of life.

So try to slowly experiment with coming out of your safety well. Take some reasonable risks. You will be amazed to find that the results of your positive moves will be mostly positive. Sometimes there will be negative consequences, but the rewards will far outweigh the negatives.

CAN'T FLY

Have you lost an ability? Are you spending your life mourning the loss?

At one time, chickens used to fly. During evolution, they lost this ability.

Roosters wake up in the morning and are the first to greet the day. They moved on with their lives. They don't complain. They don't stay in bed and sob.

Be the rooster and start greeting the world in the morning, even if you have lost something.

MATCHSTICK

Before a matchstick burns a jungle, it has to burn itself.

Before you hurt someone, you have to experience the pain of betrayal.

Before you destroy someone else's peace, you have to agitate yourself.

THE DEADBOLT LOCK

You had an ordinary lock on your house. Thieves broke in easily. You put in a deadbolt lock and the break-ins stopped.

Bad events happened in your life. You made impulsive, bad decisions. An accident, a rape, or a loss stole your tranquility in the past. Those recollections are the thieves of your mental peace. It is like the thief is visiting your house again and again, stealing your happiness. Put a deadbolt on those memories.

Realize that the event happened in the past. It is gone. It is done with. You can't undo it.

So, be wise. Put a deadbolt on your bad memories.

CHANGE YOUR COOKIE CUTTERS

If you have a star-shaped cookie cutter, all your cookies will look like stars. You want differently shaped cookies. When someone makes different dough and you cut the cookies, they will be star-shaped, too. You may wonder why it is that all your cookies come out the shape of a star... until you decide to change your cookie cutter.

Bill was eight years old when his mother developed cancer. His father was an alcoholic. His mother decided to put Bill into a boys' school. His mother explained to him that, with her rapidly deteriorating health, it was the best course of action. He remembers when he was climbing the stairs out of their basement apartment. His mother was sitting in a wheel chair. He kept looking toward her as he held his Dad's hand.

He wanted his mother to reach her arms toward him for a last hug. His mother never did and he remembered feeling extremely rejected. He wanted to cry. He wanted to wail with tears pouring out of his eyes, mouth open and distorted, but he remained frozen all the way to the boys' school. He kept thinking that his mother had rejected him.

He met his mother only a few times after that. She was rapidly deteriorating. She died soon after. His father drowned in his alcoholism. He tried to become close to many nuns in the boys' school. He adored them and tried to be a good boy. He wanted them to hug him and tell him that they loved him because he missed his mother. But they would not respond the way he wanted them to.

He is a grown up man now. He grew up with a cookie cutter called rejection. If his wife, Jill, does not respond to him the way he expects, he feels rejected. If Jill talks to any coworkers and does not smile or wave her hand at him from far away, he feels rejected.

He tells Jill that she is rejecting him. His wife has tried her best to make him feel accepted and loved. She loves him. However, Bill constantly feels that she is rejecting him. Jill is getting very exhausted. She has done everything in her power to show her love for him but Bill cannot interpret her behavior as anything other than rejection.

His cookie cutter is the shape of rejection. He is not capable of cutting any other shape like love, acceptance, or admiration like what Jill offers him. He perceives anything and everything as rejection.

Unless he recognizes his cookie cutter and changes its shape, he will not be able to accept what Jill has been offering him.

PRECIOUS MOMENTS

If you have one glass of water in the middle of a desert, what do you do with it? Do you drink it or wash your soiled feet?

If your answer is to drink it, your priorities are right. Washing your feet with that precious water would be perfectly okay in a city with an abundance of water.

Our time is like the glass of water in the desert of life. It is limited, precious, and scarce. Once a day is gone, it does not return. Once an hour is gone, it does not return. You will never be 25 years old again. This moment, once gone, will never come back.

What are you doing with this moment? Get your priorities straight.

GET OUT OF YOUR HEAD

We can stay inside the house and occupy ourselves with minutiae of daily living. We shift clutter from one side of the room to the other.

We do not recognize that it is sunny, green, and beautiful outside. Maybe we should go outside to enjoy the sunshine, flowers, and warmth.

Similarly, we can remain busy in the clutter of our thoughts. Learn to recognize these recurring random thoughts.

Say to yourself, "Stop it." Say it aloud if you are alone. Then immediately focus on the *real* things around you. Observe the physical beauty surrounding you. Think of all the real things to do and enjoy. Get out of that dark room inside your head and get into the fresh and beautiful "outside."

THROW RESENTMENT AWAY

You took your dog for a walk. Throwing your dog's droppings in a garbage bin as soon as possible would be the common sense approach! If you carry it around with you, the smell will negatively affect you and everyone who comes close to you.

Many of us carry resentment within us. Even though we have the choice of dropping it to become free of its effects, we don't. We lug this resentment with us day and night. It stinks up our emotional life.

Do whatever you can to get rid of your resentment. Talk, forgive, use a negotiator, move away, get marriage counseling, or break up.

End the resentment. Walk away smelling fresh.

WORRYING ABOUT WINTER

How wasteful and ridiculous it would be if you were to worry about the biting cold, slush, and dryness of winter while you're lying on the warm sand of a beach.

Many people fear possible future problems even though their present life is going nicely. They say, "Things are so great, but there are days that I am so afraid that something bad will happen," or, "Things are so great, something's bound to go wrong soon." They do not enjoy what life is offering them *now*.

Bad things happen to all of us. One day I am going die, you are going to die. Then our children will become grandparents and eventually die. Then our grandchildren will become old and die as well. Sure, it will happen. No one has stopped the progression of time and life. Why are you worrying about things you have no control over?

Why are you worrying about the bad? You can't stop it by worrying about it. Worrying will only cause you more stress. So why don't you enjoy the sunshine, the warm sand, and the sound of seagulls on the beach? When the winter comes, it too shall pass.

Whenever you get lost in the fear of the future, you transport yourself from now to a future that may or may not ever happen. We have no control of that in the present. You can use your today to take action that will prepare for your future. However, it's impossible to know just what the future holds.

You do have control of your present. Stay here and enjoy the moment! If you have to visit the past, visit the nice places you have been. If you want to go to the future, think about what nice things can happen. Use your present, past, and future to make you a happy person today.

CROSSING THE BRIDGE

Are you a person who constantly worries, "What if there is a bridge, how will I cross it?" You will travel the road worrying day and night without encountering a bridge. Please note that worrying about it was wasted energy.

Sometimes you worry about difficulties of the future, which never happen in the end. All that worry sucks the life out of you.

How about saying, "I will cross the bridge if I encounter one. Until then I am going to enjoy my day."

DON'T PERPETUATE YOUR OWN MISERY

Let's say that a steer hurt you with his horns in the past. But now, the steer is gone. You decide to get back at the steer by beating his dung with a stick. Stop that! You are accomplishing nothing. You will only soil yourself.

Jack remembers his lost friendship with Tom, who stole his money and his girlfriend. That was many years ago. He wants to hurt Tom by telling everyone about how Tom stabbed him in the back.

Jack is going to perpetuate his own misery by pursuing that line of thinking. Jack is taking his aggression out on steer dung. The only thing he is going to get back is dirty clothes and a bad smell.

Jack should move on with his journey and leave the steer (Tom) and the dung (his behaviors) behind.

When you realize that someone has no morals, stay away from them.

A DEAD DONKEY ON YOUR BACK

I was traveling on a donkey. One day the donkey dropped dead. When I left the donkey, I kept missing it. I was not able to focus on my travel even though I got a horse as a replacement.

A wise man met me on the way. He said, "You are still carrying the dead donkey on your back. Let it go. Move on." After that, if thoughts about the donkey troubled me, I told myself, "Why am I carrying a dead donkey on my back? Move on." The journey became easier after that.

Jessica worked. She loved her job. Her supervisor, Mary, went through a nasty divorce that changed Mary's personality. Jessica resigned and found a better job. She could not focus on her new job because she kept reliving the tragedy of her old job.

Her last job was the donkey that died. I asked her why she was carrying "a dead donkey" on her back.

Jessica let go of the mourning for her old job and moved on in her life's journey with her new job.

Always watch your back. Are you carrying a dead donkey from the past?

MY ATTIC IS FULL

Jackie hesitated when her son and daughter-in-law requested to move in due to their job losses. There was no space in the house.

Both of them worked on Jackie's attic, basement, bedrooms, and closets and discarded articles with Jackie's consent. There was so much room that they easily moved in and yet the house looked uncluttered.

Our lives become full of chores and time-consuming activities like the clutter in Jackie's house. We drive holding a sandwich in one hand and the steering wheel in the other. We accumulate activities over the years. We keep on adding more things to do without letting go of the old ones.

I remember writing hundreds of cards for Christmas for many years. I was getting tired of it. One day I decided to stop sending hundreds of the cards. Instead, I decided to reply to those who sent me a card. Those who did not send a card to me had no reason to complain. I saved at least two days of my holiday season.

Ask yourself if what you're doing is a necessary activity. What will happen if you skip it? Stop unwanted subscriptions, memberships, and activities.

I call that cleaning the attic of things to do.

EVERY DAY IS A GIFT

When someone tells me that it is a miserable, cloudy day, I respond, "Today is an appreciation day." They look at me inquisitively. I tell them, "God gave you this day so that when He brings a bright, sunny day, you will appreciate it."

In India, a cloudy day is considered a picnic day, and a rainy day is considered a romantic day. When people have only hot, sunny days, they start wishing for clouds for relief from the oppressive heat.

Enjoy each day as it comes, even if it isn't your current ideal.

FILL UP YOUR TANK

Go ahead; fill up your gasoline tank. When the gas is low, fill it up again. You do not have to buy gasoline to last you a lifetime today.

Keep your mind light by not filling it up with the solutions for every eventuality of the future. If you are preoccupied with worry, others cannot find a place in your thoughts.

Take care of essential gasoline like life insurance, long-term care, and a retirement plan. However, finding solutions for every possible event of the future will burden your present so much that you will not enjoy life.

Just as you fill up your gas tank as you travel, similarly you will know your needs as you go.

DO NOT VEER OFF THE ROAD

Jack was sitting on a train commuting from work to home. His mind started wandering, "My wife is getting old. She is developing a belly and soon I will not be attracted to her anymore. That will lead to a lot of fighting, I am sure. My marriage will probably end up in divorce. A failed marriage means I will have failed...."

When you travel on a highway, keep watch on the traffic ahead. Sometimes your mind wanders and your car swerves to the side. As a good driver, you bring it back straight on the road. If you do not do that, you will have an accident and hit a car, a tree, a sign, or an embankment.

Jack should recognize that his thinking has gone off the highway of reality-based thinking. He should recognize that he has a great job, a wonderful family, and a loving wife with whom he shares a loving and satisfying sexual relationship. He should straighten out this thinking and realize that time and age have taken a toll on both of them, not just her. Her face is not as young as it once was, but neither is his. Accepting the changes of their advancing age will bring his thinking back to the highway of reality.

Always keep a tab on your thinking. If you catch your thinking veering off, bring it back to reality.

MISPLACED FRUGALITY

Bill grew up during the depression. He would use a toothbrush until he wore out the bristles; he would wear undershirts full of holes. Both parents were very appreciative of Bill's frugality.

That was many, many moons ago. Now, Bill is the vice president of a big company. He has a six-figure income. He has misplaced his old habits about money in his current household. His meager tips to waiters have become a cause of embarrassment to his family. He gets angry that his wife does not appreciate his efforts to use the money wisely.

When will Bill realize that the dialogues of his childhood do not fit into his current life? He must start behaving like a vice president in his present. To do that, he must learn to adapt to change and different situations appropriately.

WHAT IS IN YOUR BAG?

Do you travel? If so, you must remember all the places you visited. You brought home memories in the form of souvenirs. You discarded others because they lost their significance. The significant pieces are still with you.

Similarly, our life is a journey. We travel through childhood, youth, middle age, and old age. We bring with us a part of each one of these times. At 40 years of age, a little boy or a girl remains inside you. You find the feelings of a teenager hidden there. These feelings entertain you and, sometimes, they embarrass you. Often you get scared and recoil from these feelings because you fear turning into a child again.

Well, do not be afraid. We all go through these stages. A teenager has a child and a boy in him. An old man has a child, a boy, a teenager, a young adult, and a middle-aged man in him.

Experience and enjoy the richness of your life. Do not be scared. By experiencing these feelings, you will not turn into a child. It just says you have been to those places and remember them.

DON'T SAVE FOOD UNTIL IT GOES BAD

You have food in your home but stay hungry for fear that there will be no food for tomorrow. When tomorrow becomes your today, you reach for the food. To your disappointment, you discover that the food you saved has spoiled. You did not eat it yesterday, and you cannot eat it today.

Some people worry and fear their future so much that they spend their life saving for their old age. People postpone all spending, all joy, and all vacations until retirement. They want to hold off on everything until they retire. During retirement, their health and circumstances change in such a way that they cannot enjoy their savings. Their saving for the future makes their present unhappy.

Save a little for tomorrow . . . but *do* eat today.

GET YOUR HAND OUT OF THE TRASH

If you had a choice between fishing out garbage in the city dump or cutting flowers in your garden, which one would you chose?

Obviously you would rather cut the flowers in your garden instead of sorting through smelly garbage.

Life gives us choices. You have unpleasant memories in your life. That is your life's trash. You also have your hobbies and work; those are the flowers in your life's garden. Please note that sometimes you get busy with sorting through the old trash. At that time, you forget that you have the choice of enjoying the joys of your current life.

LEARNING TO LET GO

When someone makes a nasty remark about you, do not pick it up and carry it around with you. Do not let it make you feel bad by continuously thinking about it. Continuing to repeat those words and events in your mind will only make you miserable. When someone says unpleasant things, take appropriate actions and then let them go.

While going for an evening stroll, you come across dog droppings someone didn't clean up. You don't pick it up and bring it home, right? Alternately, if you look for wild flowers and bring a bunch home, your house will look and smell nice.

If someone does or says something pleasant, keep repeating it in your mind. Tell it to others. Spread your good feelings all around. Take all the wild flowers of smiles, good wishes, compliments, and the actions of others and bring them into your home and into your life.

If you come across someone leaving negativity behind, go around it and move on.

DON'T LIVE IN YOUR ATTIC

People store old stuff in their attics.

Some of us visit the attic when we need something. Others spend the whole weekend in their attic rearranging the old stuff.

Our memories are our psychological attic. We have gotten rid of thousands of unimportant memories, like numerous breakfasts, dinners, or showers. There are some memories we do not want to get rid of. We remember events that were special to us. Occasionally we visit them because we need them to live in the present.

When you spend most of your time recalling the past hurts and joys, you have lost the ability to live and enjoy the present.

Ask yourself: Why do I spend so much of my time in the attic of my life, instead of on the main floor?

Catch yourself reliving the past. Bring yourself back to the present where you belong. The attic is for storage; you should be in your *living*room.

LIVING NOW

Doreen said, "I am 50 years old now. I look back to when I was 30; I was so young and beautiful. People used to be around me all the time. I went to clubs, danced, hiked, and played volleyball. Every time I think about those days, I get so depressed. Why didn't I enjoy them more? Why did I let them pass me by? I wish I were back in those days."

I asked Doreen, "What are you going to say about your life at fifty when you are an 80-year-old nursing home resident?"

She was very animated when she said, "I will say that when I was 50 I was working, I had a lot of friends at work. I visited family members. My friends and I went for movies often. My husband was alive and loved me so much. He could not get enough of me. I earned well and spent a lot on clothes. I had my own car. Those were the days."

When she saw her present life from the perspective of being 80 years old, she realized that she was wasting her time remembering her 20s and 30s.

From then on, she stopped talking about her lost youth and started enjoying her present life.

Know & Appreciate Yourself

ONE WART DOES NOT MAKE YOU A LEPER

Imagine that you saw a wart on your arm and self-diagnosed it as being leprosy.

There is a difference between having a wart and being a leper.

A wart is a small growth of skin that usually remains under control and is treated with pills, burnt chemically, or removed surgically.

Leprosy involves nerves, skin, the mouth, and bones. There is progressive deterioration. The treatment is complicated and involves far-reaching problems.

Our life is going well until we make a mistake. Let us suppose it is a drunken driving arrest. We start feeling bad, depressed, and inferior. Life becomes more and more difficult while dealing with the legal ramifications of having a DUI. We become suicidal; we think of going away and disappearing because of the embarrassment. In short, we see ourselves as a leper whose whole being has become bad.

At that time, it is very important to recognize that you are a good person who has done something bad. You are a good worker, father, friend, son, and husband. This isolated problem should not cast its shadow on your self-evaluation as a person.

By making one mistake I do not become a bad person. I am a good person who has made a terrible mistake. I will rectify my mistake. Keeping that attitude will help you focus on one bad habit and take care of it.

Remember; growing one wart on your body does not make you a leper, and one mistake doesn't make you a bad person.

THE MENU

Religion is like a menu in a restaurant.

Everyone likes something different and there are many options. Even though it is the same kitchen and the same cook, every one eats a different food.

Likewise, we all take away something different from religion. There are many, many religions, just like there are many dishes served in a restaurant. Everyone likes something different to eat, and everyone connects spiritually to something different.

IN BETWEEN

When a diamond is removed from a signet ring and is lying in the jeweler's box waiting to be set in a pendant, it is still a precious diamond.

Sometimes in our lives we are also in in-between situations, for example if we lose a job and are trying to find the next job. Maybe a relationship ended and we are looking for that important person in our life. Our marriage ends and we are dating, looking for the next person who could be our life partner. Our book is rejected and we are looking for the next agent or publisher. We had a fight with our spouse and are not talking to each other, waiting for things to settle down. We move from one neighborhood to another and we are friendless.

These and many more situations are in-between situations. At that time, many of us start questioning our worth. We feel worthless, unattractive, and lonely. Remember that just a few hours before the in-between situation we were feeling okay. Don't let a change of circumstance change your self-worth. You were good and you *are* good, just like the diamond. If it is waiting to be set, it does not turn into a worthless piece of charcoal. It is still a diamond. Once it gets into its next setting, it will sparkle again.

Once you find your next job, next girlfriend, next boyfriend, or next publisher, you will shine again like your usual self. Don't let the situation define you. Let the definition come from your inner qualities, your skills, your education, and your accomplishments.

IS THERE A REAL SELF

Jack sold you an iron statue painted with silver. He said it was made of silver. Jack is always anxious around you because he fears discovery. Peeled paint may reveal the reality of the statue.

Overly critical parents voice the faults they see in their children. The children learn and grow up self-critical. "I am irresponsible, lazy, and no good, so my mom is mad at me." This is a little boy's ugly self-image. He does not like himself.

He works hard, gets into sports, is a good student. He thinks he is made of a base metal like iron. He is trying to paint on a silver coating to be accepted.

He feels vulnerable to being found out that in reality he is, "irresponsible, lazy, and no good."

He works hard and attends college to become a surgeon. The fear of being found out that he is a phony and a hypocrite never leaves. He fears being rejected by his wife and friends. He lives with a feeling of dread. He shies away from people and situations that may expose his reality. He feels exhausted and tired of keeping the persona of a successful surgeon.

This surgeon has to say repeatedly, "There is no iron statue or a silver statue in me. No one made an iron statue. No one painted it silver. I am made of flesh and bone like everyone else. I had a negative childhood. Life circumstances have continually molded me. I was what I was when I was seven. Now I am what I am, 35 years old. I will be different when I am 50 and 75 years old. I am always changing. My thoughts, my actions, my values, my achievements, my skills, my relationships, and my world are changing. This is me. I am not an iron or silver statue. There is no inside and there is no outside. I am what I am."

Work on your education, your skills, and your value systems. Take it one day at a time. But don't let what others tell you define who you are.

SOUND MAKER

My wife puts on a sound maker next to her bed. It makes white noise all night so that she cannot hear the traffic outside. Thus, she is able to sleep a good night's sleep.

Please note that her reality of life (i.e. the traffic outside) remains the same. However, because of the white noise, she can improve her sleep.

Our mind has a lot of noise in it. It includes worries, undone tasks, fears, losses, and demands. We can create white noise through the company of our friends and time spent with our hobbies.

Time spent at the golf course, movies, or on our coin collection can distract us from our chronic stressors.

Switch on the white noise at night by playing golf during your stressful days.

ACT LIKE A REAL ESTATE AGENT

Have you ever gone to look at a house with a real estate agent?

He talked about its history, VIP owners, the number of rooms and bathrooms, the fireplace, school system, neighbors, and the jacuzzi. He opened the curtains quickly and turned on all the lights in the house to make it bright.

He kept you so busy with the positive aspects of the house that you were not able to focus on the negatives.

Jack had his share of problems. He dropped out of college. He began abusing drugs. He lived with his mother, who had become wary of his problems. His mother continues to criticize him and mentions his past failures during conversation.

Jack felt that he has moved on, but mom is stuck to her picture of him when he was having all those problems. I suggested to him that he had to learn from the behavior of the real-estate agent. He should treat himself as the house and the mother as his buyer.

As soon as he entered the house he was to highlight his achievements of the day. In addition, he would appreciate what his mother had done. He started thanking her for little things she did including cleaning the house or cooking. He would tell her all about what was happening in college. As the time passed, his mother started to ignore the negatives and began talking to the family about Jack's college and the promotion at his job. Jack made a sale of his changed life to his mother.

If *you* wouln't sell you, who would?

A MERCEDES BENZ

A Mercedes Benz was so proud of herself. Everyone looked at her with pride. She always felt that she was a mark of quality.

One day she found herself surrounded by Ferraris, Rolls Royces, and Lamborghinis. She started feeling like a junk car. She forgot that she was still the same Mercedes. If she went on the highway, most of the other cars around her were less expensive and not as well-made as she was.

Joanne was very proud of the fact that she finished her master's degree in communication. She was one of the best students in her college and was the pride and joy of her teachers. She found a job in a large publishing house and was surrounded by very talented and knowledgeable people. Sometimes she feels inferior and insecure. She compares herself with only those people around her who are her superiors. She does not realize that, in a few years, she will be where they are. She forgets that ten years back these people were in her situation.

She should recognize that she is still a Mercedes even if Ferrari and Lamborghinis surround her.

SCREWDRIVERS

You offer a flathead screwdriver to Joe, who is fixing something. He says, "I don't want it." It does not mean that your screwdriver is bad. It only means that you have a flathead screwdriver and Joe needs a Phillips. An hour later Joe is going to call you and say, "May I borrow that screwdriver now, please?" This time he needs a flathead screwdriver.

You interviewed for a job and were not selected. You felt rejected. "I am no good. No one wants me. I am never going to an interview just to be rejected again." You took the rejection personally and put yourself down. Maybe you are a flathead screwdriver! If you keep going to your next interviews, you will find an employer who might say, "Where were you all this time? I was looking for your skills and could not find them."

It is important to recognize what your skills are and to sell them where the market is. If you don't go for interviews, how will they find you (you flathead screwdriver!)?

A CAULIFLOWER VS. A ROSE?

A cauliflower is edible and fills the stomachs of the whole family, but a cauliflower given to a sweetheart can have dire consequences. A rose looks beautiful and can bring a smile to the face of a sweetheart. A rose is not edible, though, so trying to feed it to your family wouldn't be a good idea.

People are like roses and cauliflower. They have their own strengths and are effective in certain situations. It is very important that a person recognizes his strengths and weaknesses.

DO YOU FEEL INFERIOR?

You have two eyes; others have two eyes. You have one nose; others have one nose. You have two ears; others have two ears. You have two legs; others have two legs. Yes, everyone around you looks similar.

Likewise, you may have a fear of abandonment; others have it, too. You may have feelings of inferiority; others do, too.

We are human beings with universal emotions. Do not make the mistake of thinking that everyone around you feels secure and you are the only insecure person.

No one is inherently inferior or superior.

THE WISE DO OTHERWISE

Some people put their unusable furniture, knick knacks, and books on the curbside in the garbage. They think that because they have no use for these things, no one else will have use for them, either.

Other people understand the inherent value of things so they arrange a garage sale. In other words, they have all their junk neatly arranged on the driveway with a garage sale sign.

People who visit the garage sale look for treasures. I recall a friend who bought a book of mint postal stamps for $50. My friend found that the cost of the stamps if used as postal stamps to mail letters was more than $200.

Jim is very quiet. He feels inferior and thinks he comes across as a weak person. He feels inferior to his brother, who is a big talker. Because he does not talk much, he listens. Nevertheless, people like Jim more because he is a good listener.

Alternatively, you can be like the second person. Instead of devaluing your physical, psychological, ethical, or spiritual attributes as inferior, put them out for a garage sale. By this I mean relate to people without reservation. Let people look at you and evaluate. They may like your looks, demeanor, personality, and other characteristics.

Rediscover yourself with an open mind. You will be amazed how many people like you just the way you are.

IF YOU WANT TO FLOAT, GRAB A LOG, NOT A ROCK

A rock is bound to go to the bottom of the sea and take you with it. However, if you hold on to a wooden log, it will help you stay afloat.

When you have a crisis in your life, do not cling to your friends who are themselves having problems. They will introduce you to *their* solution, no matter how bad it is. They are themselves drowning and will take you down with them.

Let go of your friends with alcoholism, drug addiction, and criminal problems. They are the rocks who will take you down with them.

Hold on to people around you who are sober, clean, working, and stable. These people are like a log of wood and can help you to stay afloat.

ONE MAN'S TRASH IS ANOTHER MAN'S TREASURE

One day you looked in your attic, garage, and basement. You took out all the stuff you have accumulated over the years. You wanted to put it out on the curb as garbage. Instead, you did a garage sale. People came and bought a lot of the stuff that you were ready to throw away.

Now think about your attributes that you don't like. "I have acne scars on my cheeks. I am shy. My butt is too big."

Well, put it all out there. You will be surprised to find that many people see qualities and attributes in you that you never appreciated or were ready to throw away. Stop apologizing for yourself and start living with pride.

I PAY MY BILLS

I asked hypersensitive Beth, "How come others' opinions don't bother you anymore?"

She replied, "They do not pay my bills. I do not have to care what they say."

When you say, "I pay my bills; I don't have to care what they say," you have changed your self-talk, your sub-vocal talk.

Try it. You will find that this simple sentence will often stop that self-loathing inner talk about why people are right in putting you down.

YOUR BEST FRIEND IS YOU

When you run into a friend, you smile, shake hands, give gifts, and make each other laugh.

Now let us see how you treat yourself!

You have worked hard and attended to your business to the level of exhaustion. However, you berate yourself for not completing the task early. You put yourself down for not finishing tons of undone work. YOU don't let yourself sleep.

Are you your own enemy?

I think you deserve a thank you, some rest, or some cold tea on a hot day to soothe you. You deserve a manicure, a massage, a dinner at your favorite restaurant. Give yourself the gift of chilling out and not doing anything on a Sunday. Watch a favorite movie with your head resting on your partner's lap.

Most of all, when you see yourself in the mirror, smile and greet yourself warmly and enthusiastically. You deserve to treat yourself as well as you treat your friends.

You are your best friend.

OPINIONS ARE COOKIE-CUTTERS, YOU ARE THE DOUGH

Have you seen someone make cookies? They start with a flattened sheet of dough. They punch out a shape with a cookie cutter. If they go to another sheet of dough and make more cookies, the shape of the cookies remains the same.

People are like cookie cutters in how they see you. You have much more to offer in the world, but other people have a limited ability to see all of your good qualities or full potential. Some people have *no* ability to see the positives. They may be depressed themselves. They are critical of themselves and others around them. They always find faults in you. Do not believe them. These are the people who do not like the shapes of the cookies they see.

Always remember that a cookie cutter is limited in cutting only one shape, even though the dough is ready to be cut in thousands of ways.

Always remember, you are much more than just what others can see in you.

WHAT'S IN YOUR STORE WINDOW?

People look in a store window, get interested, and walk in. They browse the store. They walk out with good, neutral, or bad feelings. They decide to revisit the store depending on how they felt looking at the merchandise inside the store.

Your personality also has a window. You display your personality with an eye contact, a well-articulated hello, your telephone greetings, and the way you dress.

Once people come into your life, they see your sincerity, trustworthiness, value system, and stability of your relationships. That is what makes them revisit you and become your friend.

On the other hand, a nasty remark or poor eye contact can easily turn important people off. They don't enter your store. Even if your personality is very good, they never get the chance to know you because they don't like what's in the window.

I AM WHAT I AM

People put hurdles in their own way. They do so by saying derogatory things about themselves. These statements may have a little truth in them, but the rest is false. A man in his forties said, "I want to go to college, but I am not sharp anymore."

There is an iota of truth to this. The 40-year-old man is not as sharp at picking up new facts as he was when he was younger. On the other hand, he has matured now. He is serious about his education. He has the ability to go back to college and earn his degree. The man should say to himself, "I am what I am. I have to do the best that I can with what I have." He can then join a college with full awareness of his abilities and limitations.

Whenever any deficiency seems to stand in your way about your looks, your age, your family, your ethnic background, or your intelligence, do not feel paralyzed. Accept yourself by saying, "I am what I am," and move on to your next project. Do not let doubt cripple your continued progress.

BECOMING SUNSHINE

To light up a dark room, you have to turn on a light.

On the other hand, the sunshine never waits to be turned on. When the sunshine finds windows, doors, gateways, holes, and cracks in walls, it lights up the room without a formal invitation.

Some people are like light bulbs. They wait for an invitation, an initiative, an approach, a hello, or eye contact before they start a conversation. They are afraid of rejection. They want a guarantee of acceptance by others.

On the other hand, there are people who are like the sunshine. They do not need a request. These people are the first to say, "Hello." They make eye contact, smile, and offer a compliment. They do anything and everything to take the initiative of making an acquaintance and beginning a new friendship. They are the sunshine and light up our lives.

Next time you meet someone, stop being a light bulb. Become a beam of sunshine in their life.

BE YOURSELF INSIDE & OUT

There were two shopkeepers with stores next to each other. Ronan spent lots of time decorating his window. He had insufficient merchandise in his store, but whatever he had, he would put in his window. Every week he would decorate his windows in a daring style.

David spent most of his time taking care of his merchandise inside the store, but never decorated the window. He believed that his customers would know the high quality of his products and that flashy window trimming was excessive. At the end of the year, Ronan sold double the amount of merchandise than David.

Some of us show our caring in words, deeds, or gifts. We say, "I love you," "Thank you," or give compliments. When we do that, we are acting like Ronan who dressed up his window regularly. We bring out and show what we have inside our hearts.

Others want people to automatically understand and know their feelings. They find verbalizing their feelings of love and affection to be a superficial act. As time passes, important people pass by them without ever knowing their feelings. Yet, they expect affection and love from others without first expressing their own. They are disappointed without ever realizing that window dressing is as important as the richness of their heart.

If you love someone, don't be afraid to say, "I love you." Tell them through your smiles, eyes, kisses, gifts, cards, flowers, chocolates, handshakes, and hugs.

THE ROSE BUSH AND THE MAPLE TREE

One morning, the prince of a kingdom walked into the royal garden. He looked at a rose bush. "This plant is covered in thorns," he said with disgust. "It can't even provide shade. This is a worthless plant." He then stood facing a maple tree. After a quick assessment he groaned, "This tree doesn't grow any fruit. Hmm... another useless plant, I see." He ordered the gardener to remove both of them.

The prince's harsh comments hurt the rose bush and the maple tree. They felt sad, inferior, and scared.

The king and the queen visited the garden at noon. The scorching heat made the queen feel faint. The king sat her down to rest in the shade of the great maple tree. The king spotted the beautiful and fragrant blossoms of the rose bush and ordered a bouquet made for his wife. As soon as the queen saw the bouquet of flowers, a vast smile spread across her face.

The king winked and smiled at the handsome, tall maple tree and the beautiful rose bush. He announced that the two plants never be cut down because they served the royal couple well.

You will encounter people like the critical prince who will only point out your flaws. These people will make you feel inferior. You will also meet people like the king who will appreciate your positives and make you feel good about yourself.

It is very important that *you* know your strengths as well as your weaknesses. If you are a rose bush, don't try to become a maple tree. Even if you magically did, you would lose your fragrant blossoms. If you are a maple tree and you try to become a rose bush, you will lose all your relaxing shade.

Do not panic when criticized. An admirer may be right around the corner.

Dating

EXCLUSIVE RESTAURANT VS. PIZZERIA

Let's say you went on a date to an exclusive restaurant. Your date summoned the waiter and pointed out water stains on the plates. He commented that his knife and fork did not match. He returned the pasta that was not cooked *al dente*. He remarked that the waiter was inept and apologized to you. He complained to the manager about the poor service he received.

Your next date took you to a pizzeria where the food was served on plastic plates. Your date was genuinely happy to meet you. His eyes sparkled as he savored every morsel of the pizza and every word of your story. The evening passed by swiftly. As you stepped out, he remarked that the pizza was great. You said, "Yes, it was!" even though you didn't recall what the toppings were.

You enjoyed the pizza place more. It was free of criticism and judgments. It was full of genuine interest.

Just because something is exclusive doesn't make it better. Your first date wanted everything to be perfect and complained about minor issues, while your second date was full of joy and good conversation. So, what do you prefer: an exclusive restaurant full of judgment and people who think they're better than everyone else? Or a fun night out at a pizza place enjoying great conversation?

HAILING A CAB

You want a cab. Some unoccupied cabs don't stop for you. You have this nagging feeling that for some reason they don't want you. If you are black, Jewish, younger, sport long hair or a goatee, you think that is the reason. It is very important for you to realize that as much as you want the ride, the cabby wants a passenger. The next unoccupied cabby is glad to see you and stops for you. Those who did not stop for you had their own reasons. Some were off duty and were heading home. Some were rushing to pick up a designated passenger.

Now let's apply this concept to dating. You are single and want a boyfriend. It is like waiting for a cab on the street of life. It seems as if all the men are taken. You get attracted to Ron who seems uninterested. Tom is on the rebound. Bob turns out to be gay. Harry is just not ready to settle down. They have their own reasons. They are not ready at this time. There is nothing wrong with *you*, though. So keep your goal of finding a good boyfriend and keep circulating until you do.

Do not get discouraged; keep hailing the people you like and one of them will be glad to see you and stop for you.

ARE YOU IN THE MARKET FOR A HOUSE?

Look at many houses. Some houses look very good from the outside. When you go inside, they do not serve your needs. Once you find a house you like from the outside and the inside, purchase it.

People are also like houses. Some look very good from the outside. While dating, if you find problems of alcoholism, drug abuse, physical or emotional abuse, or a personality incompatible with yours, avoid him. If he brings a lot of garbage from the past into the relationship, move on. In summary, if you end up becoming unhappy relating to your date, there is a problem. Listen to your gut.

Do not knowingly settle for a defective relationship when you have the choice of looking for others.

DO NOT GET ATTACHED TO HOTEL ROOMS

On your vacation, you stayed in a hotel room. You came to the room just to change clothes or to sleep. The rest of the time, you had fun at the beach, sightseeing, or meeting new people.

Sometimes people attach themselves to their hotel rooms. Either they get very distressed by small flaws in it, or they attach themselves to the room and feel pain when leaving.

When dating, we meet men and women. Dating is a process of eventually finding a mate that you could live with, enjoy a long-term relationship with, and marry. Some people react to every dating experience as if it were a marriage. If the relationship fails to go forward, they feel destroyed, become very upset, feel rejected, and vow not to date again.

Recognize that dating is a process and that many relationships will come and go before you eventually settle down with one person. Think of these smaller relationships as hotel rooms on your vacations. The goal was not to enjoy the hotel room but to enjoy the vacation.

Here, the goal is to enjoy the process of dating like a vacation. The people you dated and moved on from were the hotel rooms of your romantic life.

A NEW TAKE ON LONELINESS

"I broke up with Jane. I will never, ever get involved again. It's just too painful. I can't take being rejected. I have had three relationships and they all ended in agonizing breakup! I feel lonely whenever I see couples."

Let me ask you, what do you do when you buy a shirt? Do you blindly go into the first shop, walk up to the first rack, and pick up the first shirt you see?

Of course not!

You look at many shops and shirts before you buy a well-fitting shirt you can afford. You take so much care in choosing a shirt. You must work even harder when selecting a life partner.

Dating is a process of elimination by which trial and error leads to a final selection of a partner. During this process, you are trying different partners. No one means to hurt anyone. If they accept each other because of insecurity, it would destroy their future lives. If a relationship does not last, it is better that it broke now rather than after marriage.

Please don't hesitate to walk away if things aren't right. On the other hand, if your partner feels that her chemistry does not interact with yours, it is better that she lets you go. She is doing you a favor.

One day you will meet someone with compatible chemistry and both of you will click.

COOKING SPAGHETTI

It is impossible to cook a pot of spaghetti without putting heat underneath it. If you put water and spaghetti in a pot and expect it to cook with no heat, it is not going to happen.

Your fantasy is to meet someone attractive, sexy, well-balanced, loving, well-employed, and comfortable. You want to meet, date, go steady, get engaged, and get married to someone without the tribulations of dating!

Chances are very slim that will happen. Meeting, dating, building, and breaking relationships are part of the life of a maturing adult. Each time you meet someone, you mature as a person until finally you find someone you want to spend your life with.

That is almost like having the heat under the pot of spaghetti. Just as the spaghetti will not boil without heat, a good relationship will not come your way without the heat of the dating game. Some of it is exciting and some of it is painful.

Just as heat is essential to cook, the uncertainty of dating is essential for final discovery of that lasting relationship. The more you put the fire under the spaghetti, the tenderer the spaghetti becomes. If you play it safe and keep the spaghetti in safe, cold water, it remains useless for eating.

Being a Better & Happier You

AVOID THE SNAKE, CHANGE THE PATH

A man goes to his work daily and encounters a snake on the way. He is afraid of being bitten by the snake. He discovers that other roads also lead him to his work but they are without any snakes.

People are stuck with a bad boss or colleague in a job. They are so stuck to the job that they remain miserable.

Recognize that there are other jobs available and that changing your job could free you from a mean boss or colleague and send you on your way to more happiness in life. Change the road you're on and get away from those snakes.

EVERYONE HAS DIFFERENT TALENTS

Is a diamond or a sapphire more beautiful?

The answer to that question is either, depending on the setting in the jewelry and what someone considers beautiful. Either of them can look more beautiful if the jewelry is designed well. Some people also prefer sapphires to diamonds because of their color.

We know people with high intelligence, academic performance, or professional achievement. On the other hand, we know persons with average intelligence who may have other talents and skills.

Who is successful in life as a human being depends on how they fit in with rest of *their* world.

You have heard of crazy genius. You have heard of mean, filthy rich.

Nevertheless, you choose a moderately successful friend to spend your vacation with when given a choice.

Don't feel inferior if you are not the "best." Give equal attention to how you fit in with your social, family, and professional environments.

RECTIFY YOUR WRONG DECISIONS QUICKLY

When you take a wrong turn onto a dirt road, you quickly return to the highway before you get lost or trespass on a large rural property. Come back to the main road to travel towards your goal.

On the highway of life, we make wrong decisions. Whether it is the wrong career, relationship, habit, or addiction, take action to come back to a better life as soon as possible. The longer you stay on the wrong path, the more difficult it will be to rectify the mistake. You could get lost on a back road you don't really want to be on.

Apologize as soon as you can if you have hurt someone. The longer you take, the more anguish and hurt both of you will face. If you take too long, hesitation will develop and you will get lost in the woods of negative feelings.

A SNAKE CRAWLS OUT OF ITS SKIN

A snake crawls out of its old skin by growing a new skin first. The old skin sloughs off its body and the snake crawls right out with a new, shiny skin.

The same applies to us human beings. Our old habits are our old skin and difficult to get rid of. Let us develop new habits that will replace the old, unwanted habits.

Imagine that you drink several cans of beer while watching TV. You recognize that it is a bad habit, but still that is what you do every night. To break the old habit, go to the gym and spend more time exercising. Before you know it, your new habit of going to the gym will replace the old habit of watching TV and drinking beer. You will shed the old habit and emerge with a new, healthier habit instead.

TOO LITTLE OR TOO MUCH

Jane grew up eating unsalted food cooked by her hypertensive mother. She did not like the unsalted food. Once she started her family, she made sure that there was salt in whatever she cooked. She didn't care about putting other spices in the food. "Mom," her daughter said, "it's tasteless and too salty!" Jane shouted back, "Quit! You're always complaining."

Jack grew up in poverty with an alcoholic gambling father. Jack was often hungry during his childhood. He resolved that his children would never be hungry. His wife complains that he is not available to help her in the home, attend a parent's day in school, or go to family gatherings because he works too much. He tells his wife that she is a complainer.

Note that Jane and Jack both have lost their ability to find a balance. Too much or too little salt, both make cooking inedible. The same is true about work. Too little or too much work both make for an unhappy life.

A balanced work and family life is the key to happiness.

HONEY BEE AND HOUSE FLY

A honeybee buzzes on the flowers. A housefly is attracted to trash.

Keeping this in mind, there are two kinds of people.

The first are those who notice goodness in others. The second are those who only notice others' faults.

What kind of person are you?

THE LEECH

Leeches attach themselves to people and animals to suck blood without the knowledge of the person. You have to pull it off if one attaches to your skin.

A worry can be like a leech that sucks your energy without your knowledge. You have been repeating the same problem. You have tried to focus on answers.

You have to say, "This is a worry. I am not solving any problems. I have a mental leech sticking to me. I have to get rid of it."

Only by examining your body can you see a leech sticking to you. Similarly, only by examining your thought patterns can you recognize the worry leech draining your energy. Ask yourself what you are worrying about these days. Be honest with yourself.

You will be able to recognize many worry leeches. Get rid of them.

YOUR ANGER IS LIKE GASOLINE

A gasoline can destroys itself and anyone around it if ignited. The same gasoline used in machines will give heat and electricity.

Gasoline can destroy or be a constructive force, depending on how you burn it.

Anger is like gasoline in you.

When you are angry, your immediate tendency will be to yell curses and teach a lesson to whomever you are angry at. If you burn it by blowing your top, you will hurt everyone around you.

Be wise and use your anger to rectify injustice. Hold your temper. Ask yourself what you can say and do to use the energy to fuel a constructive course of action.

DROWN IN SIX FEET, PLAY IN FIVE

Joseph is a high-powered attorney making six figures a year. He has worked very hard in his life and enjoyed his work and family.

Recently, he has been thinking about retiring at the age of 55. He keeps calculating how much he will need to live on. He talks about cutting down his lifestyle. He says he will stop staying in five-star hotels and his wife can stop her antique doll collection hobby. The more he thinks, the more agitated he gets.

He wants to write and spend more time with his wife and children. Life seems to have passed by. He feels that he has succeeded professionally but lost out on personal joy. He also mourns the loss of his professional success if he retires when he is at the zenith of his carrier. Here is the metaphor that helped him resolve his dilemma.

Imagine that you are in a swimming pool. The water has risen to exactly your height. It is suffocating you, choking you, and drowning you. You have the following choices. You can continue to stay in the pool and try to enjoy swimming while being afraid of drowning, or you can get out of the pool and not come back. You could also reduce the level of the water to five feet and continue to enjoy swimming.

It was easy for Jack to see his black and white thinking and resolve his professional burnout problems. He spoke to his partners and worked out a new schedule, making more time for his wife, children, skiing, and writing. The reduction in his earnings has been minimal because he still works full-time.

Removing excess water leaves it at a depth that is great for swimming but does not drown him. If you are professionally burned out, see what you can do to remove some of your work schedule or rearrange it in order to enjoy more personal time.

LIFE IS A ROSE BUSH

If you stick your hands in a rose bush and get thorns in your hands, you will cry in pain.

Alternately, you can carefully avoid the thorns and pick out a beautifully fragrant rose from the top, keeping you safe from the thorns.

Some people form relationships without much thought. They let friendships develop by chance. It can result in pain and tragedy if you pick up an unknown person in a bar without knowing his background.

Some people observe others carefully in social situations like work, church, social meetings, etc. They find out more about them before opening their hearts to them.

You may avoid active drug addicts, alcoholics, gamblers, and abusers who can give you a lot of heartache.

Don't make impulsive decisions. Take time to observe and make a rational and educated decision about who you let into your life.

BLOOD-SUCKING TICKS

Ticks stick to your body painlessly. You don't even know that they are there. They suck your blood and pass germs and disease into your body. It is very important that you look at yourself after a walk through the woods and ask someone to look at your back where you can't see. Remove any ticks sticking to your body.

In the same way, we pick up bad attitudes and habits while going through our life. These attitudes and habits suck our spiritual energy without us even being aware of it. They can make us pessimistic and bitter about life.

It is important that we look at ourselves in an impassionate way. We can also ask our friends, priests, or therapists to help us look at the blind spots in our personality and bad habits we've picked up along the way.

See if an "attitude tick" is stuck to you.

A BUCKET OF WATER ON YOUR CAMPFIRE

Imagine that you are lost in the woods. It is cold and you know that, unless you build a fire, you are going to freeze to death. You go around searching for precious sticks of dry wood and then you light up a flame. It gives you life-preserving warmth. As you sit there, your body warms up and the shivering stops. Suddenly the smoke from the fire burns your eyes. You get angry. You pick up a bucket of water and throw it on the fire. The flames go out, leaving only rancid smoke. As you start shivering with cold again, you are unable to rekindle the fire and you almost freeze to death.

Similarly, Joe's life was going on well. One day he got angry because his boss made him angry. He stopped at a bar on his way home and got drunk. While going home, he got into an accident, received a Drunk-While-Driving ticket, lost his license to drive, and lost his job. That started multiple problems with ferocity.

Next time when you get angry, stay away from impulsive actions that could add new problems to your life.

DON'T STARE AT GARBAGE

You go for a walk and notice some rotting garbage someone left on the sidewalk or in the grass. It is unsightly, nasty, and disgusting. You keep walking and see flowers in your neighbor's yard. You chat about the blooms. You come home smiling.

Bad and good things happen to all of us. That is life.

You may focus on hurts and nasty things, or you can focus on the good things in life. The choice is yours. Walk away from nasty interactions and events as soon as you can. Soon good things will happen. Spend your time and attention on those.

The choice is yours. The result is yours, too.

BE YOUR OWN PUBLIC RELATIONS MANAGER

Organizations hire public relations companies to get feedback from their customers to rectify problems. I can describe the defects of my mother, father, brother, cousin, teacher, wife, and son. I can also tell you when and how each one of them has hurt me. It is so clear in my mind.

What I don't know is *how I have hurt them.*

Once we realize that we are also capable of hurting others, we can work on bettering ourselves. Ask people, "What do I do to upset you?" Make sure that you don't respond with instant explanations about why you do these things.

Become your own public relations manager by actively asking feedback for your performance as a boss, father, brother, husband, and employee.

BUILD A STRONG FOUNDATION

A bad builder gets so lost in the beautification of the house that he neglects pouring good concrete in the foundation. He builds a beautiful house, but after a few years, a crack appears in its foundations. It is beautiful but not fit to live in anymore.

If you want to be emotionally happy, strengthen your life's physical foundations. The body is physical. In this physical body lies an organ called the brain. The mind, emotions, and psyche are the functions of the brain.

Love, affection, happiness, thinking, problem-solving, creativity, romance, and sexuality are functions of the brain. To make your brain a healthy organ, you have to eat well, sleep well, keep a daily schedule, and exercise daily.

If you do the above five things you will have a rock solid and stable foundation of your brain and thus your mind.

HOW MUCH GUILT IS GOOD?

Guilt is like table salt. A pinch makes the soup taste great, but a spoonful makes it too salty.

A little guilt makes us reliable, truthful, law abiding, and honorable. Too much guilt makes us hate ourselves and resent others.

Use a pinch of guilt, not a spoonful.

FLYING PHOBIA

While flying over the Atlantic Ocean, I had a thought. What would happen if the airplane broke into pieces? After falling for 15 minutes, I would hit the surface of the water and bob up and down in the massive waves. The water would fill my lungs and I would drown. As I pictured it, I felt the choking sensation in my throat and chest. I looked around. My wife was sleeping with her head resting on my shoulder. The man next to her was eating peanuts. The woman next to him was reading the in-flight catalogue.

I was the only one imagining falling out of the sky, screaming, yelling for help, and fearing drowning. The plane had been flying for ten hours. I thought of the flight attendant who had spent every working day of her life on flights. She was alive. I thought of the pilot who had been flying airplanes for the 30 years. That was his chosen profession.

I was making myself miserable by visualizing those scenarios. What made me miserable was not the airplane flight, but my own worry and self-talk. Once I realized it, I calmed down and fell asleep with my head leaning against my wife.

Next time you feel scared during a plane ride, watch out where your mind is going.

DO NOT BREAK YOUR CLOCK

You are in your deep sleep when the unpleasant alarm wakes you up. You get very irritated and curse the clock. You hit the snooze button every five minutes. You pray that the five minutes pass slowly. At that time, you deny that you are the one who wants to wake up in time to catch a flight. Your relationship with that alarm clock becomes that of a child and a parent.

It is true in our lives, too. We have goals to achieve. We communicate our goals to our loved ones. They give us feedback, direction, and suggestions. They criticize us for our mistakes. At that time, we act like the kid and the alarm clock. We resent their reminders and their criticism as personal attacks. We forget that, like the clock, they are our tools. We had set them to help us reach our goals in our life.

Next time someone criticizes or reminds you, remind yourself that it is your clock helping you to be punctual and stay on track to reach your goals.

STEER CLEAR OF DRAMA

In the journey of our life, we meet people who involve us in their conflicts and negative thoughts and feelings. They stink up our lives.

Think of a time when you were walking on the sidewalk and saw dog droppings in your way. What did you do? You stepped around or over them. Now think of another person who sees it but steps right into it.

Do not let other people's drama stink up your life. Watch! Do not step in it.

Do what you can to help, but try to stay clear of their negativity.

WHAT IS YOUR NONVERBAL MESSAGE?

What would you do if I gifted a pitcher of water to you? What would you do if I brought you a hammer? What would you do if I brought you an umbrella?

Each object has a silent message. The pitcher says, "Here I am full of water—drink from me." The hammer says, "I can take care of the nail problem." The umbrella shouts, "It is raining, open me and protect yourself."

Like the objects, we also send silent messages to people. Some of us give a message that we truly want to give. We are able to change our message according to our needs. These people have realistic communication. However, some of us unintentionally give faulty nonverbal messages.

Let me give you the example of Joyce. She has been married twice and is in a relationship with a third man, her present boyfriend. She has the same complaint about all of them. Men are emotionally and physically abusive and violent. I ask her, "Why did you stay in a relationship with your husband who beat you up daily?" Her answer was that her children were small and she did not want him to leave. When I asked, "Why did you take the abuse from the second one?" She replied that financially she was hard up and could not have survived without him. "And the current abuser?" Her health is very poor, she needs insurance and that is why she stays.

She gives abusive and manipulative men a message that says, "I will stick around no matter what you do." She teaches them how to treat her.

If she recognizes and improves the silent messages she conveys, men who aren't abusive will be more attracted to her while men who are will be less likely to see her as an easy target. She must learn to send out a silent message of strength and self-respect, not desperation and need.

STOP AT A GAS STATION

If you are lost, stop at a gas station and ask for directions. Change your course and reach your destination.

If you lose jobs, get in to debt, or break up with your significant other, ask yourself, "Am I taking the right path?" It could be a serious problem. Whatever the path you are taking, it is showing you the unwanted results.

You have to stop at a gas station of life and ask for further directions. Alcoholics Anonymous, Narcotics Anonymous, Gamblers Anonymous, a credit bureau, or a counselor can change the course of your life.

Recognize that you are lost. With the right guidance, you can reach the destination of happiness and success.

$2 ROSE

The florist buys long stem roses for 50 cents apiece. Then he shaves off its thorns, selectively removes its unnecessary leaves, and sets it in a vase. He can now sell it for $2.00.

You are also like the rose.

Look at yourself critically. Do you have thorns? Do you yell, get irritated, use abusive language, make impulsive decisions, or have unclean habits?

Please work on them to become more dependable, pleasant, courteous, and thoughtful. Wear a bright smile. You will be amazed to see the difference. People will seek you out for friendship, business, and relationships. Trim away your thorns and unnecessary leaves.

HOBO GUESTS

You wouldn't let a smelly hobo sleep in your bed. That is how it should be. Only your friends and loved ones should enter your home. Only your lover should stay in your bed with you.

Your mind is like a house. When you think of your child, you let him in the playroom of your mind. When you think of your boss, you entertain him in the living room of your mind. When you fantasize about your lover, you let her in to the bedroom of your mind. You let people enter your mind where and when it is appropriate.

Sometimes you let your ex-boyfriend from your past live in the bedroom of your mind.

Please recognize and expel the memories of people who do not belong there. They will repeatedly knock at the doors of your mind. Do not let them in.

Watch for unwanted guests in your head!

IS THE SOFA YOUR BEST FRIEND?

I turned on the TV and there was a nature show on called, "Wild Dogs." In one scene, a wild dog was chasing a rabbit. The rabbit scuttled down a rabbit hole, and for the next several minutes, I saw the dog trying to scratch out the dirt and reach the rabbit. His lunch, I guess.

In the meantime, I saw my dog, Chewy, sitting on the sofa next to me. His eyes were shut and his breathing was slow. He had just come from the kitchen where we keep his water and food bowls always full.

I kept on looking at the dog on the screen trying desperately to get at his meal and back at Chewy, who eats without ever hunting.

This comparison lit up a light bulb in my head. Human beings in the past did physical work for their food, just like the wild dog.

Now, we have a friend called Mr. Sofa. Now we order pizza while sitting on a sofa. We get it delivered to our doorstep. We eat the pizza sitting on a sofa. We read on a sofa. We do leg lifts, thinking we are exercising, on a sofa.

No wonder there is an epidemic of obesity with half of Americans being overweight.

It is time to change friends; the sofa isn't a very healthy one.

APPLY MAKEUP TO YOUR PERSONALITY

I have been amazed to see the transformation that eye makeup can create. Women enhance what is naturally there. The eyelashes become thicker and longer. The eyeliner defines their eyes and the shadow brings out the brightness of their eyes. Their plain eyes suddenly appear large, luminous, and beautiful.

You can also apply makeup to your personality. You have natural attributes; start enhancing them.

Smile more earnestly by letting your teeth show, jaw relaxed, mouth open and eyes partly shut. Say hello in a confident and well-articulated voice. Make eye contact and make it last longer when you conversate. Shake hands with firmness and hold the person's hand a second longer.

Give a gentle squeeze with a hug, and let go after a second longer. Instead of just saying thank you, send a short hand-written note.

Just enhance what you already do. You will be amazed to see the warm reaction these small enhancements bring in those around you.

Apply makeup to your personality.

START A VIDEO COLLECTION

Our mind is a like a video recorder. It makes video tapes of our experiences. These become memories.

People replay the video tapes of childhood physical, emotional, or sexual abuse. They replay arguments between their parents. They replay their negative perceptions of their siblings treating them unfairly. When they replay these memory tapes, they feel sadness, anguish, depression, anxiety, anger, jealousy, and resentment.

Now let me turn to your unhappy memories. I am sorry that bad things happened to you. We cannot change that. What we can do is to increase the library of your new positive, joyful, and peaceful experiences.

Let me share with you a few of my calm scenes.

One morning, I saw flower-laden branches of a dogwood tree outside my window. They were swaying in the breeze. The gentle back and forth movements made me feel calm.

I was 13 years old. My aunt had a baby. Around 1:00 PM every day, she sang a lullaby to put him to sleep. I would look at the calm and peaceful face of the baby as his eyelids slowly became heavy. My aunt would gesture to me and we would both tiptoe out of the room.

My family visited a beach. In the morning, we had our breakfast of eggs, toast, and tea on the terrace of the hotel. We could see the beach, hear the seagulls, and smell the salty sea breeze.

I have many more of these calm scenes in my memory. During a busy day, I close my eyes and start my mental video tapes to see those calm scenes.

Make a permanent recording of what gives you pleasure. Later, play back these calm memories. The more you occupy yourself playing happy scenes, the less time you will spend watching the unhappy parts of your life.

THE BROKEN STATUE

One day I found a replica of Venus de Milo made of plaster of Paris in my attic. I recalled that we bought it 25 years ago. My wife wanted to buy one. However, we had a two-year-old son. I warned my wife that the statue was top-heavy and would fall and shatter easily. I warned her not to be upset if it broke.

We drove home and parked our car at the curb. My wife carried our son and I carried the statue. I put it down in the living room and returned to the car to bring in our remaining things. When I returned to the apartment, I saw that the statue was broken into pieces. My wife was upset and our son was crying. The joy of buying that statue was gone. For the next few days, both of us felt sad.

Somehow I was able to fix the broken statue. My wife sprayed it well and it became like new again. Every time I looked, the statue reminded me of my sweet son crying. We kept that statue in our living room for many years and then put it in the attic.

Our distress about the broken statue was a complete waste. I am sure that if we went back in time, my wife would treat the broken statue differently. We made our son cry for a statue, which has been gathering dust in the attic for years now and is of no importance to us.

Before you explode, ask yourself, "How will I feel about this in 25 years?" Reevaluating the loss from a different perspective redefines its impact.

Go into the attic of your life; look around for the evidence of wasted precious moments. Discover how you fretted about some petty events. Modify your reaction to present losses with your wisdom from the attic. Looking at past mistakes can make you value your present relationships more.

THE FARMER WHO BECAME RICH

A farmer bought a hen and a rooster. He made sure that the hen sat on her eggs to warm them for 21 days. Soon more eggs hatched and he had more hens and roosters. Before you know it, he had a large poultry farm and lived happily from the income generated by hatching eggs.

The positive thoughts in your mind are like the high quality hen's eggs. Do not let them stay there cold. Soon they die and are of no use to you or anyone else.

Hatch them into spoken words. Once hatched, they produce a good effect on others and yourself. People usually return compliments with their own words and actions. That, in turn, creates more positive thoughts and feelings in your mind and heart. Make sure that if you get a positive thought about someone, hatch it.

Speak up when you like something about your dear ones.

Before you know it, you will have a lush farm of good feelings, thoughts, statements, and deeds.

KEEP THE BUTTER AWAY FROM THE OVEN

The farther away the butter is from the heat, the better the chances are that it will keep its form. If you bring it close to a heat source, it will start to melt.

Like butter, we are vulnerable beings. It helps to know our weaknesses. This will allow us to avoid risky situations.

These weaknesses can be food, alcohol, sex, drugs, gambling, stealing, or shopping. If you stay away from the people, places, and things where you are likely to engage in such activities, it helps you to remain solid instead of melting and giving in.

Remember, you are a solid block of butter and can remain so, as long as you stay away from the heat of your weaknesses.

HUGS & KISSES OR HI & BYE

We relate to many kinds of people in our life. Some are a source of happiness and others of unhappiness. You wonder, "Why is it that I am doing every-thing right, but with each passing day, this person becomes angrier with me and ignores my efforts to be close?" This person ignores all your efforts. The lack of positive response makes you feel a lack of control. You start getting angry or depressed.

Previously you used to greet the person with hugs and kisses. You used to have the kind of chat that stems from a close relationship.

This is the time to change from a "Hugs & Kisses" relationship to a "Hi & Bye" relationship.

Now when you run into this person, say, "Hi," to them. Then get busy in your business. Talk to other people. You smile and say, "Bye," when it's time to leave. Less effort into the relationship reduces your expectations as well as the pain of that loss of closeness.

THE WORLD IS AN ECHO VALLEY

There was a valley surrounded by tall mountains. We used to yell, "Hello!" It was fun to hear our own words come back to us. "Hello . . . hello . . . hello. . . ."

Once I felt that people were not responding to my greeting. I thought about it. I soon realized that my face had grown very serious. My smile and hello were so faint that the other person could not recognize my greeting. He only saw a flicker on my face which he could not figure out.

I suddenly remembered the echo valley. To hear a hello, we had to yell our own hello loud and clear.

I started saying, "Hello," more loudly, with a big grin on my face and a wave of my hand. Since that day, when someone walks towards me, they smile and return my hello without fail.

Initiate greetings loud and clear if you want people to greet you in return.

IS THE SOUP TOO SALTY?

Relationships can become disagreeably salty, just like soup.

A patient came to me with depression. She and her husband were friends. They had fun until the children were born. Now the only thing they had to do was work and care for their children and the house.

There was no more fun.

There was no more joy.

There was too much "*have-to-do* salt" everywhere around her.

When soup is too salty, my wife puts in half a teaspoonful of sugar. It takes care of extra salt. We enjoy the soup, which could have ended up in the drain, wasted.

I found out that my patient dropped her four-year-old off at nursery school at 9:00 a.m. and picked him up at 11:30 a.m. I asked her, "What do you do with this time?" She said, "Nothing specific. I straighten up the house." I suggested that she join a gym. She started working out for an hour in a calisthenics class. She made new friends and started to feel physically fit. She and her husband had enjoyed ballroom dance lessons for their wedding. I encouraged them to go back. They signed up for dance class at the local high school.

These teaspoons of sugar, i.e. exercise and dance classes, lifted her depression by adding some sugar to the too-salty soup of her life.

You cannot take the salt out of a soup, but you can add the sugar.

THE BARBER CANNOT CUT HIS OWN HAIR

We may be excellent at sorting out others' problems, but we are limited when it comes to sorting out our own. Our blind spot is not visible to us and that is why we call it a blind spot. You are like the best barber in town who needs someone else to cut your hair.

Open up to a close friend, spouse, clergy member, or mental health professional. You will be amazed to see that solutions to your sticky problems and conflicts will become more easily visible to you.

ARE YOU AN OCTOPUS OR A TURTLE?

An octopus has many tentacles. Wherever it goes, it wraps them around objects. It remains restlessly engaged in anything and everything. It floats restless in the deep waters. In the same sea, there are turtles that live on the ocean floor. They keep their head, arms, and legs inside their shells. They meditate most of the time. They pursue the activities of walking and swimming only when necessary. They do not wrap themselves around objects for the fun of it. They are content in themselves.

Do you know that turtles live for more than 100 years?

There are people who are like the octopus. They are distracted and tangled up in everyone's problems. They entangle themselves in every situation like conflicts of politics, work, society, and their families. You will find them arguing with others frequently.

Other people are like turtles. They keep their pace slow. They only attend to whatever is necessary. They spend their time relaxing, meditating, gardening, reading, and chatting with their family. They live a peaceful life.

Who are you? Are you an octopus? Or are you a turtle?

DRIED ROSES

Your lover brings flowers for you. They are a joy for a few days and then they wilt. The petals fall off and you throw them in the garbage. Try something else. Next time when they start wilting, tie them together and hang them upside down in the sunshine. Slowly, these roses dry up and keep their beautiful shape. You can use these dried flowers to make beautiful arrangements or potpourri.

Every time you look at them, you recall the evening when your lover gave them to you. You recall and experience the romance and fragrance of the fresh flowers.

Life blesses us with beautiful moments. Mostly we let them go and never remember them again unless prompted. All of our sweet past memories are our cherished possessions. Do not let them pass by. Preserve the ticket stubs if you attended a concert and keep them in a scrapbook or journal. In your lonely days and dark moments, take out that scrapbook and review your mementos. Revisit your vacation to Las Vegas or dancing at your son's wedding. You can enjoy these moments repeatedly.

Your memories are like the sun-dried roses.

TRAIN TRACKS

Have you noticed that there are many tracks at a train station? You will notice that all the tracks are functioning. Trains come and go in both directions. If one track is defective, the trains are routed to other tracks.

Life also has many tracks. There is a track of being a friend, a spouse, a parent, a colleague, a coworker, a sibling, a child, a lover, and many more. Sometimes one of these tracks becomes defective.

Let us suppose that you develop a back injury and you have pain in your back constantly. You cannot go to work because you cannot sit or stand for too long. You can no longer participate in athletics or certain sexual activities. Sometimes, people shut down completely. They focus on that track and stop giving their loved ones attention. They discontinue their hobbies and education. They bring all of their feelings and thoughts, other than the pain, to a standstill.

Do not let that happen.

Keep your relationships as a friend, spouse, parent, etc. intact as much as possible. You may not be able to do as much as you once were, but you can still reach a compromise and try to maintain a number of activities with your loved ones. They will understand if you aren't able to do *everything* you could before. However, if you shut down completely, they will begin to build up resentment toward you.

Keep as many tracks moving as possible. Your life will slowly begin to move on, in spite of one damaged track.

A BALL OF CLAY

You give a ball of clay to two people. One may complain of how much dirt it is creating in their room. The other person knows exactly what to do with the clay. She works with it and makes a statue. Before you know it, she has made a piece of art.

Life gives all us 24 hours in a day. This period is like the ball of clay. Some people complain about boredom and having nothing to do. They look at their watch wondering when it will be time to go to bed. Others jump at the opportunity each day brings to them. They complete projects, plan, play, and enjoy time with family and friends. They wish there were more hours in the day.

Next time you get that ball of clay, make a masterpiece out of it.

A DEBIT CARD IS SAFER THAN A CREDIT CARD

A debit card is a convenience so that you can spend your money in the bank with a card instead of a check or having to withdraw cash. You can spend only what you have in the bank, not a penny more. You never end up spending what you do not have and cannot afford. A credit card, on the other hand, allows you to spend money that you do not have.

An ordinary person can feel happiness only if real things happen. He feels happy when he gets a job done well, gets a paycheck, celebrates his birthday, or gets a gift. If nothing special happens, he feels ordinary.

His experiencing happiness is like a debit card. He can experience happiness only if he deposited some happy deeds into his account, resulting in joy.

Think of someone who uses credit for happiness. He feels bored and uses drugs to get happy. He cashes in the neurotransmitters in his brain that were reserved for the next week. He feels really good even though it was an ordinary day. The truth is that such behavior leaves his future happiness in shambles, just as borrowing money by using credit cards may leave your future finances in shambles.

When a person continues to borrow excitement from the next month's supply of neurotransmitters, he may "go over the line of credit" in their brain. A time comes when the cocaine or scotch doesn't do anything. They need more and more to get the same high. Eventually they come crashing down, often with depression.

Learn to be content with your ordinary happiness; it will last you for a long time. Do not use drugs and alcohol. It will create deficits of happiness because of excessive borrowing.

FILE IT AWAY

Sometimes you come across papers that are not urgent. You can attend to them later. You neither throw them out nor do you leave them to clutter up your desk. Instead, you file them away. They stay in your file, secure. When you have a few minutes, you take them out and work on them.

At bedtime, the undone work, the incomplete projects, the difficulties of the day, and the deadlines clutter your mind. Adrenaline surges through your body and keeps you from getting tired. You toss and turn in your bed all night. You do not solve any problems during the night. You get out of your bed in the morning with a headache, feeling tired and anxious. Instead of having solved your problems, you have created a new one: sleeplessness.

Try using the "file it away" concept. When you are ready for sleep, sit down at the edge of the bed. Ask yourself, "Is there anything urgent that I need to attend to before going to sleep?" If the answer is yes, get up and take care of it. If the answer is no, then put a paper and pencil on your night table. Mentally file all of your worries, concerns, fears, and problems away until the next day. Some things may pop into your head in the middle of the night and wake you up. Rather than lying awake and dwelling on it, write it down on the paper. Tell yourself that you have filed it away and then deal with it in the morning. Keep your mind's "desk" free of clutter and you will sleep well.

THE CATERPILLAR AND THE BUTTERFLY

Caterpillars live in cocoons that keep them warm and safe. They eat a little food and stay cramped in the cocoon. They grow and get wings. Eventually, the caterpillar cuts through the cocoon and emerges as a butterfly. It flies into the fresh air and sunshine. It tastes the delicious nectar from the flowers.

Another caterpillar in a cocoon sees the butterfly and says, "Come back here, sister. Do not fly into that sky. You will fall and break your wings. A bird will come and eat you. Come back here into the cocoon and you will be safe."

The caterpillars that come out of their cocoons and become butterflies live a life of excitement. Birds eat some, but the rest go on to live their life flying. All of the caterpillars who are too afraid to cut themselves out of the cocoon die there and never taste the nectar from the flowers.

When you try to grow, go distances, and take risks, your loved ones become anxious and fearful.

Sometimes, though, the people around you may not even want to keep you *safe*. What they really want is to keep you *the same*.

Think of the husband and wife who are alcoholics. They have been hiding in a cocoon of alcohol together. When one of them decides to break out of the cocoon and become sober, the remaining spouse may be frightened of their partner's sobriety. They offer their partner drinks and encourage them to stay in the cocoon. They undercut their partner's attempt at sobriety so that they will come back and give them company. Remember, the caterpillar feels the warmth of the cocoon, but never the warmth of the sunshine.

Fly out of your cocoon. Taste the nectar of life.

Working Toward Success

OPINION OR COMMAND

"My father says things that are so crazy I get really angry. I don't want to talk to him. Later, I feel guilty for avoiding him and start listening to him again. Then I get mad again. Hence I go through these cycles of anger and guilt. What should I do?"

During childhood, his word was a command for you. If you did not obey him, there were real consequences. His statements were absolute orders.

Times have changed. You are not little any more. Your food, shelter, and money does not depend on him.

When he gives his suggestions and opinions, you automatically hear them as commands from your childhood. That bothers you because if you do not listen him, there will be dire consequences.

That is not true anymore!

Remember that you are grown up. Nothing of importance really depends on him. This is America and everyone has an opinion. Even a drunk on the street has an opinion.

Your father is not giving a command. He is giving an opinion. It is up to you to listen or not.

THE JUICY MANGO

A woman from Haiti once told me a story. She was very fond of mangoes as a little girl. One day she stood under a mango tree eyeing a really juicy, ripe mango and wished it would fall. She went every day and stood there looking at it. One day, her dream came true. The ripe mango fell but it struck her left eye. She had excruciating pain followed by a hospital visit. She has had pain and vision problems in her left eye since then.

Is a dream-come-true always good?

We work hard to achieve success. We saw success from where we were. Once we reach our destination, we see the landscape in reality. Marriage brings its struggles. A job brings its responsibilities. Stature brings limitations of movement and action.

The girl did get the mango but she also got the black eye. It is very important to be ready for the unexpected. Be prepared to deal with the unexpected and to recognize that even a dream-come-true can have its setbacks.

THE HORIZON

As a child, I believed that the sky and the earth met behind our school building. As I grew older, I went to the back of the building. Then, I thought that the horizon was at the border of the town. The more I walked towards the horizon, the farther it moved away from me.

We say to ourselves, "Someday I will start it."

Life's mundane problems keep us busy. We say, "As soon I get time I will start it."

We watch time pass by, slowly and steadily. "Someday" remains as elusive as the horizon.

That someday will come as soon as the pressure of the job is over, the little babies grow up, the teenagers have moved on to college, or retirement comes.

"Someday" never comes. It looks close, like the horizon behind my school building. But "someday" does not exist. Only *today* exists.

WARM HANDS

When two hands rub against each other, both hands become warm.

If you are a boss, a teacher, a parent, or in any kind of leadership position, you need to improve your organization continually. It does not matter if your organization is your family, your business, or your soccer team.

You must recognize that the people who report to you are full of ideas. Too often, those in power dole out advice and give their opinion but forget to seek the opinions of others to improve their organization.

Ask for their opinions!

You will benefit in a number of ways: You will improve your organization, but you will also make those you're in charge of feel very good. They will be proud that their opinions matter. They will feel that they are part of the team, not just a cog in the wheel. Don't forget to give credit where credit is due when ideas come from someone else.

It does not make you look small. The fact that you can benefit from someone else's ideas confirms that you are a good leader. Also, your family, team, or employees are more invested in the company or team because their ideas are making a difference.

By encouraging input from others, both hands become warm through working together.

WHEN WALKING, LOOK FORWARD

Those who do not see where they are going trip and fall. They stumble on sticks and stones. Those who look in front plan to scale big mountains and don't trip along the way.

Look ahead if you do not want to fall and fail in your life. You can look ahead even at the present, which is the road immediately ahead of you.

Those who are always engrossed in their past memories, resentments, guilt, hurt, failed expectations, and unfulfilled goals cannot focus on the road ahead.

Remain in the present and look forward to the future.

LIFE IS LIKE A GAME OF BASKETBALL

Players run after the ball and take the ball to the net. They use all their skill to get the ball. The struggle and the spirit of competition make the game interesting.

What would you think about a basketball game where players willingly gave the ball to the other side and they did that to avoid hurting the feelings of other players? The game would become boring.

In our life there is also a symbolic ball. That ball can be a job opening or a girl you love. You feel guilty taking the job so you let your friend take the job. Later on, you expect the friend to be thankful to you; he says that he got it because of his own efforts.

After someone wins a game of basketball, he does not want to hear that the ball was handed over to him. Of course, you have played it wrong by letting your friend have that job. Don't be afraid of competing.

Remember! Giving away the ball is called game fixing, which is illegal.

THE BUMP ON THE ROAD

One day I hit my head on the ceiling of the car while driving. It was a sudden shock and painful. I stopped to find out what happened. I found an unmarked speed breaker on that road.

An unmarked speed breaker can create an accident. It is good to know that there is a bump ahead.

It is also good to know that there is a bump on life's road ahead. Financial stresses like student loans, weddings, birthdays, illnesses, and breakups are all bumps in the journey. Brace yourself for them. Taking precautions such as opening an education account and having long-term care insurance can take the surprise away from the bumps on life's road.

Look ahead in life.

Look for the bumps and prepare to deal with them.

YOUR CONTRIBUTIONS COUNT

You have to open your mouth to get your dental cleaning. Without your cooperation, the dentist cannot do his job.

Your contribution is important in any relationship. Don't become inactive if someone else has the major responsibly. Your cooperation can make the project go faster.

Joe was hoping to become the project leader. When Jim led the team, Joe became inactive.

Jim asked him how he would feel if the situation was reversed.

Joe became aware of his sullen attitude. He became more cooperative and Jim recommended him for the next leadership position.

A good leader is a team player first.

FOLD THE UMBRELLA

You cannot have a good shower if you keep an umbrella open over your head.

If you want the water to clean you and if you want to feel the temperature on your body, you have to fold the umbrella.

Jim went into his new job with reservations. He wanted to watch and observe before he put himself out and gave 100%. His reserved attitude and caution made him an uninvolved person during the administrative meetings. His boss observed him closely. Jim's credentials had impressed him. After seeing Jim in a couple of meetings, he put him down as an average employee.

Even if you are in a job or a relationship temporarily, give 100% of yourself. You never know what may come out of it.

Fold the umbrella. You don't need to guard yourself from getting wet in a shower.

THE LANES OF THE HIGHWAY

It is not necessary to travel in the left lane if you feel uncomfortable in it.

We are all different. The pace of life is different for each of us. Some of us are naturals in a fast-paced life. Some of us dislike the physical and emotional pressure. You can move into the middle lane or the right lane if that's the case.

They all reach the same destination.

Working slightly less hours or less rapidly can take away pressure from your life and achieve similar objectives that we would have gotten by over-working ourselves. Whether you become a workaholic or stay more relaxed, the road will still lead you to your destination.

TOSS A PENNY IN

You say that you want to be a millionaire, but you don't make that kind of money. You spend whatever you earn.

While you are reading this book, walk over to your kitchen, pick up a cup, and throw in a penny.

You are already on a journey towards becoming a millionaire. Write down 999,999.99 dollars to go. Each time you throw in your change, write down the balance. As the time passes, you will start putting nickels, dimes, and then even dollars into the cup.

The same is true about learning a new skill.

Maybe you don't know how to work a computer. There is a hidden statement attached to this one: "I am not going to learn the computer."

If you are someone who isn't computer savvy, ask someone you know to teach you how to turn the computer on and off. You have put a penny in the cup of "computer know-how." Congratulations!

The next day, ask them to teach you how to read news on the computer. That is a nickel of computer knowledge.

Next is email. That is a dime of computer knowledge.

Before you know it, you will be an expert "millionaire" of computer knowledge.

KEEP THE ROADMAP IN MIND

There are many kinds of roads and trails throughout your journey. There are clearly marked highways like "Washington Highway South to Washington."

The signs clearly guide you to your destination. There are roads with names, but you don't know where they take you, like Maple Avenue. Finally, there are unmarked trails in the woods and back roads. It is easy to miss a trail and get lost in the woods. The farther you walk in your frantic state of mind, the more lost you get.

In our life, there are different roads, too. If you take a medical, dental, nursing, engineering, law, plumbing, or electrician course it is like a well-marked highway. Once you enter it, you reach your destination by following the signs.

There are roads that are well-marked but you don't know where they take you; for example, a BA in Elizabethan History. You know what you did but don't know where it is leading you.

There are unmarked dirt roads and trails, like wanting to "experience life." You hang out and hop bars. Maybe you live in your car or couch surf for a while. You are lost in drinking, partying, and making friends with others who have no idea where they are going.

Sometimes, you realize that you are wasting your time. Other times, you never come back. You get lost in the jungle of drug abuse, alcoholism, gambling, and crime.

Watch your life's roadmap. Choose well-known highways and avoid unknown dirt roads. If you happen to start down an unknown road, come back before you get completely lost.

CHANGING LANES

You drive down the highway anxiously, wanting to reach your destination. You are driving in the left lane. If someone slower is in front of you, you get upset.

The other alternative is that you switch lanes as needed. You remain relaxed, knowing that all lanes take you to your destination.

In life, people want to achieve certain goals like wealth and social and professional success. Their motivation fires them up so much that they resent anyone who seems to be in their path.

Then again, others are much more flexible and keep multiple channels and paths open in their life. They change their styles, tactics, jobs, and professions to reach their destination. They succeed without harassing others.

Stay flexible but never lose sight of your destination.

WAVES OF THE SEA

There is a saying, "Opportunity knocks but once," but I feel that opportunities are like waves of the sea hitting the shore. The longer you sit on the shore, the more waves you will see.

The longer you stay involved with life and people with an open attitude, the more opportunities come your way. Every day, every relationship, and every problem is an opportunity to grow and move forward in your life.

If you believe, "Opportunity knocks at the door but once," you will miss the *new* opportunities. You will be like a person who went to the beach, saw one wave, closed his eyes and refused to look at the next wave.

Those who react to lost opportunities with guilt, remorse, and anger miss the waves of opportunities that continue to wash ashore.

THE STORY OF THE KING

I remember reading a story about a king whose sole concern was to make his people happy. He did everything in his power to make his people feel happy.

One day a man came to his court and complained, "We have no place to live and you have such sprawling royal gardens." Therefore, the king ordered his men to open the gates of his garden to the public. People came and set up camps there.

After a few days, another man came to court and complained, "I live with my whole family in one room while you occupy an entire palace." Therefore, the king opened the doors of his palace to his people and moved into one room.

A man complained that there were not enough rooms in the palace and his family needed a place to live. The king gave up his room and moved out of the palace. Now the king had nowhere in his own kingdom to live. Someone was occupying every bit of space; hence, the king went to live in the forest.

After a few days, a woodsman came upon the king and demanded that the king leave because he was disturbing the forest. The king felt so helpless that he declared he would kill himself. The woodsman complained that the king's dead body would take up space in the forest and that was unacceptable to him!

The king began to cry. Suddenly there was a *"POOF!"* When the smoke cleared, God was standing before him. God said, "I sent you to this earth to give them leadership, to keep law and order so that they could live in peace. Go and see what you have done. There is chaos in your kingdom. You were supposed to run a kingdom well, not keep everyone happy."

The king recognized his mistake. He went back to his palace and ordered it vacated. He worked hard to restore order to his kingdom without concerning himself with each individual person's happiness. Soon, the kingdom was running smoothly and the people tolerated their own occasional unhappiness.

In difficult situations, remember this king. You don't have to make everyone happy; it's impossible. Instead, remember why you're here and do what needs to be done to maintain order and peace.

THE BLUEPRINT AND THE HOUSE

An architect made a blueprint for your dream house. The blueprint has been sitting on your desk. Months pass by; you do not have a house. The blueprint is not enough. You have to *build* the house.

Your desires and wishes are like the blueprint from the architect's office. You can sit on it for years without executing it. If you really want to build your body and lose weight, you will have to take action. Having the desire is not enough. You will come home every day from your office with the blueprint to exercise but end up sitting in front of the television. Remember, a blue print helps you to build the house one brick at a time.

Go ahead and start working on your goals.

AIRPLANE FOR SUCCESS

Let us suppose that you and I start walking towards Florida. After an hour of walking, you decide to take an airplane. I continue to walk. You will be in Florida in a few hours while I will be just a few miles away from where I started.

Both of us work. Both of us want to reach higher in our company. You decide to join college part time and get a degree, while I continue to work hard in my job.

The company selects you as the vice-president and I remain a manager.

Go back to school! It's like catching a flight to success.

LEARN WHAT YOU CAN

You have to dig deep into a coal mine and shovel tons of coal to find a few diamonds.

The same is true about Alcoholic Anonymous meetings, Narcotics Anonymous meetings, and college classes. Not everyone who gives you knowledge knows how to teach. Patiently listen to what people say and extract what is useful.

When it comes to people, you also have to sift through ample coals of information to find a diamond. Be patient. Keep going to classes and meetings to look for those occasional pieces of useful information. You never know what great things you'll find.

GET INTO THE RIGHT LANE

You may be out of the work force because of an illness or childcare costs. The idea of rejoining work frightens you.

It is as if you developed a phobia of getting back into the left lane of the highway. First, recognize that you have developed a fear. Then accept that you can overcome your fear.

Enroll into college. Make sure you take the easiest course you can find in the brochure when you first start. Next semester, join another course you think you can attend. Join a volunteer group that relates to the field you are interested in.

That is the right lane of the working world.

Soon you will lose your fear and will be able to apply for a job, the left lane of the highway of life.

UNPLANNED EXITS

If you are studying for an examination or preparing for a project, keep your destination clearly in your mind. Make plans for limited breaks. Do not take unplanned breaks to watch television or spend time on a phone chat or emails.

Jack's goal is to reach Washington D.C. He starts at 7 AM. He plans to have his lunch at 12 PM. He has two breaks to refuel and to have tea. He reaches his destination at the right time.

Now think about Tom who gets distracted by fixing a broken door handle that he could have postponed. He leaves at 10 AM. He exits from the highway because he sees signs for a war museum and a flea market. He loses his way in an attempt take a short cut. He misses his appointment in Washington D.C.

Unplanned distractions steal your precious time and can make you miss your deadlines.

REACH YOUR DESTINATION

Think of a person who wanted to go to Washington D.C. He carelessly picks up a map that reads Washington. Had he looked carefully he would have seen that the map he was reading was for Washington State. He will drive for hours without reaching his destination.

You may have great aspirations and goals. If you do not plan and execute carefully, you don't reach your destination. Your lifestyle will lead you to a different destination.

Those who plan their life's journey carefully will achieve what they desire.

THE PUDDLE

You were born in a poor family, had an ordinary education, and had an ordinary job. Yet you have the capability of having big dreams, goals, ideas, and read books by Plato and Aristotle. No one can control your dreams and goals.

One day, I saw the reflection of the moon and stars in a puddle of muddy water on the road. It struck me. Even though it was a short-lived muddy puddle, it had the courage of reflecting the moon and the stars.

You may be a puddle of muddy rainwater, but you can reflect the moon and the stars, too, if you choose to do so. Don't be afraid to dream big.

DID YOU FALL?

If you fall from the back of a horse, you can do one of two things. You can choose not to ride a horse again or you can choose to get back on the horse.

The same is true about remaining sober, being punctual, and being faithful. If you want to be sober, get back on the horse of sobriety even if you fall off.

Visualize a horse. Whatever your horse is, keep getting back on it. Do not give up. Get up after each fall and keep trying.

TALENT DETECTOR

There are three kinds of people. The first kind is unaware of the ground in front of him and if a lost coin is lying in his way, he walks right past it. The second constantly scans the ground in front of him and often finds lost money. The third kind uses a metal detector. He scans the lawn, the beach, and the local parks to dig up lost jewelry and coins. The more he finds, the happier he becomes.

Let us compare the person who finds metal objects with the person in life who finds positive qualities in others.

There is the first person, who does not notice goodness in others even if that goodness is right in his face. The second person recognizes and compliments a good job or an outstanding performance. However, the third kind possesses a behavior metal detector. He goes out of his way to look for the positives. He notices small improvements, digs up talents, and compliments them.

By digging out buried qualities and talents, he makes other people realize their hidden potential. He is the leader that inspires everyone.

A TORNADO OR AN APRIL SHOWER?

A tornado is roaring, devastating, injuring, killing, uprooting, downing, and destroying everything in its path. When April showers come, they bring relief from drought and heat. They water the plants, grow greener grass, wash away pollen, and replenish lakes and rivers.

People may enter an organization like a tornado.

Their selfish agenda guides their relationships. They step on everyone else's toes to get what they want. Once gone, they leave emotional and moral destruction behind them. It is impossible for other people to survive in the midst of this tornado, and often the destruction left behind is difficult to repair.

People who enter an organization like April showers come in with an even temper. They listen. They help recognize problems. They rectify the system and, by doing so, spare individuals from destructive criticism. They reward and appreciate good behavior or a job well done. People look forward to meeting, talking, and being with them. If they leave, the people left behind cherish their memory.

Are you a tornado or an April shower?

UNCUT DIAMONDS

A diamond in a coal mine looks like a chip of glass. The diamond does not sparkle. Someone has to spend a lot of time to cut the facets and polish it to bring its brilliance to the surface.

Similarly, when you discover a new interest, it is like discovering an uncut diamond. If you do not work at it, nothing special happens to it. On the other hand, if you give attention to it, work on it, get training and guidance to develop it, only then does it sparkle like a diamond.

Whether it is your interest in music, gardening, golf, or bodybuilding, you have to put focused attention into it. Only then will your interest and talents come to fruition.

Having potential is not enough; goal-oriented hard work is vital to turn it into a talent.

DIAMONDS NEED POLISHING

A diamond is very shiny. Yet you will notice that the jeweler rubs it with a polish cloth to bring out its sparkle before showing it to you.

No matter how good, educated, and ethical we are, we can always polish our knowledge. We can make ourselves better-looking, more effective, and more current in our knowledge.

Go to the local high school. Take a dance, language, computer, or exercise class. Learn how to practice karate. After a course, you will come out sparkling like a diamond.

The next time, go for a higher course.

With age and time, you will shine more as long as you attend adult education classes and practice self-study. If you do not do that, the dust of boredom will gather on your personality.

DID YOU LOSE A GOLDEN OPPORTUNITY?

You get a chance but cannot benefit from it. There are many distractions in your present life. You feel sad, angry, and frantic that you missed the boat. You tell yourself, "I missed a golden opportunity."

The next time you think that you have lost a golden opportunity, keep your spirits up. There may be a "platinum" or "diamond" opportunity waiting right around the corner. The saying, "Opportunity knocks but once," is too limited. To a person who continues to listen, opportunities will continue to knock at the door. Be sure to listen and open the door when you hear it knocking.

Jack had put his house up for sale. Days and weeks passed by and he kept decreasing the price of the house, hoping to sell it. When a customer decided not to buy his house, Jack felt very discouraged. He thought he had lost a golden opportunity to sell his house. He removed his house from the listing. He hoped to improve it and put it back on the market later. While he was improving the house, the market turned. There was a boom in the real estate market. His house went for 50% more. That is what I call a platinum opportunity which followed a lost golden opportunity.

ARE YOU PLANNING A SKYSCRAPER OR A SAND CASTLE?

An architect spent 20 years of his life constructing a skyscraper. His friend decided to build the world's greatest sand castle. Both spent energy, dedication, time, and money. It took the same number of people to accomplish their goals.

Do you know what happened? The sand castle vanished in the wind and the skyscraper lasted for over 100 years.

When you study, go to a college, hang around with your friends, or meet people and network, ask yourself, "What am I going to accomplish over a period of time?" We all have the same 24 hours in a day and a similar number of years to live.

Emperor Shah Jahan built the Tajmahal. Thomas Alva Edison invented the light bulb, recorded sound, and the movie camera. They left skyscrapers behind. Many billions of people before us have left billions of sand castles that have disappeared, leaving no trace of their work or impact on the world.

When you set a goal for yourself, ask yourself: "Is it a sand castle or a skyscraper?"

THE SNAKE AND THE EARTHMOVER

A snake and an earthmover became friends. An earthmover is a gas-propelled vehicle. The earthmover bragged that he was powerful and could move large stones, boulders, and heaps of dirt easily. The snake wondered about the power of the earthmoving machine. He was so humongous!

The snake and the earthmover decided to race across the jungle. The snake started crawling. Wherever it found a hurdle, it would go up, around, or through it silently. Despite the stones, logs, and grasses, the snake reached the end of the jungle. The earthmover crunched, destroyed, pulverized, cut, and pushed its way. Before it got halfway through the jungle, it was out of gas and one of its wheels was broken.

Going through the jungle of an organization, the person who moves around like the snake—adjusting himself to situations, people, rules, and regulations—comes out the winner when compared to the person who locks horns with every challenger.

ARE YOU A PIECE OF PAPER FLYING THROUGH THE AIR?

Have you ever seen a small piece of paper fly in the wind? It goes up, down, forward, and backward. Sometimes it falls on the ground and then goes back up in the air. It has no direction of its own. The wind takes the paper wherever it blows. Now, look at a bird. It stays in the air, the same as the paper, but it knows its destination. It flaps its wings against the wind, because it has a goal to pick up seeds for its babies and return to its nest.

There is a man who joins a college because his father tells him to do so. He has no goals. He does not attend his classes, spends his time sitting in a bar, hanging out, drinking, or using drugs late into the night and sleeping all day. He is like a little piece of paper in the wind. Wherever his friends tell him to go, he goes. How long they tell him to hang out, he hangs out. He has no goals so he will reach nowhere.

Think of a person who wants to become a pharmacist. He joins a college, studies, works, and exercises to keep his body and mind healthy. He is like a bird who knows where it is going.

Stop being a paper in the air. Start acting like a bird and know your destination.

A FISH IS A GOOD SWIMMER EXCEPT OUT OF THE WATER

A fish swims inside the pond. It goes up, down, left, and right. It dances with joy. It is confident in the water. Sometimes a fish becomes so joyous and sure that it flies up and out of the water, landing on the stones. When it flies out of the water, birds snatch it up.

We are good in some and bad in other areas. Often people become so confident in one area that they generalize this confidence to other areas without first developing the right skills.

A very good doctor earned plenty of money. He started fast food stores on the side. He had no time or expertise to supervise his new businesses. Soon he lost money in the stores. A wise person knows both his strengths and weaknesses. Success does not blind him.

If you become overconfident and jump out of your area of skill without question, you may end up like the fish. Knowledge of your skills and limits pays in the long run!

EVERYONE IS AHEAD OF ME

Do you know of any marathon runner who walked the minute he was born? No! Of course not.

Do not forget that when you are learning something new, you are like that newborn baby. You will fall many times as you learn to crawl. You may even get hurt and cry, but remember that you are in the initial part of the learning process. Do not compare yourself to others who are already marathon runners when you are just beginning your journey.

Remember that they were crawling at one point, too.

Continue on your course to learn and practice. Be patient with yourself. You have to learn to crawl before you can walk, and walk before you can run.

HAVE A PLAN

If you drive aimlessly for ten hours and put 400 miles on your car, where would you be by the evening? Somewhere around ten hours from when you started, but who knows where you would be located at that point?

But if you decide to drive to Washington, D.C., you can put those same 400 miles on your car and be in Washington or somewhere closer to your destination by the evening, *simply because you had a plan.*

I want to stress that you must know what your goal is. Unless you define your goal, all your hard work is useless. If *nowhere* is your goal, then that is where you will be at the end of your journey.

IT'S A BUMPY ROAD TO SUCCESS

The reasons for not trying are usually a fear of failure and the pain and hurt that will come from it. Nevertheless, it is important to *try* if you want to succeed.

Without the attempts, we have failed anyway.

I remember participating in my first public speaking attempt in medical school. I stood in front of an audience of 100+ students. They were a noisy bunch. I forgot the speech and they booed me off the stage.

My friend said, "Never am I going to do this again." He had been booed off, too.

I thought, *Well, I succeeded in registering my name and I have learned that next time I must use a written outline.* After three unsuccessful attempts, I won a prize. Now I am a good speaker.

Highlight your success. Ignore your failures. Keep trying so that you can keep learning.

Mindset

UNIVERSITY OF LIFE

When someone deceives me, I can't get over it. If someone overcharges me, I get so upset I can't let it go.

One time a new customer ordered supplies from my shop to deliver to her business address. She paid me by check. She asked me if I could cash a check of $35 for her which she needed for the cab home. The cab driver would not accept a check.

I gladly gave her $35 for a check. The next day, both checks bounced. She never meant to buy any supplies. She had come and wasted my time only to get $35.

We pay tuition fees for attending classes but sometimes we also learn a big lesson by paying someone for something in the University of Life. Walk away rich in experience in human relationships.

Every time someone uses a newer way of making a fool out of you, consider him your professor. Walk away wise after having paid that fee. It will hurt less and be easier to deal with and get over.

CONNECT DOTS

"My life is very limited. I do not do anything."

Fill a piece of paper with dots from top to bottom. Each dot represents activities, friends, relatives, hobbies, places, and things. Then draw a big dot in the center. The large dot represents you.

Now connect the big dot to a small dot that is next to it. That little dot represents brushing your teeth. Connect the large dot to another dot. That is you and your shower. Connect to a third dot. That is watching TV. Connect to a fourth dot; that is putting on your clothes. Connect another dot; that is your aunt visiting you.

Think more.

You read a book, so connect another dot. Keep doing it. You will be amazed to see how many activities, people, and things are already in your life.

Now start looking at other people and discover activities you can do to connect more dots. Say hello to someone in the supermarket and connect another dot. The more dots you connect, the richer your life becomes.

You can also do this same exercise when trying to make new friends. Ask yourself whom you have said hello to or exchanged a smile with. Then ask yourself who you have conversated with, spent time with outside of work, or hang out with on a regular basis.

Draw a small circle around a dot for each person you say hello to. Then draw two around dots representing whom you have friendly conversation with. Draw three circles around those with whom you spend more time.

You will notice that there are acquaintances and friends in your life. The more you relate to someone, the darker and bigger that dot becomes. By relating more frequently and by doing more activities together, you can increase your friendships.

Acquaintances are the foundation for future friendship.

You can turn an acquaintance into a friend by planning activities and conversations you both like.

Remember, everyone is looking for friends. Just the way you are looking for friends, they are looking to you to become their friend.

THE BOUQUET OF FLOWERS

Someone brings you a bouquet of beautiful flowers. You put it in a glass vase and soon the buds open up and begin to blossom. This fills the room with a wonderful fragrance. After a week, the flowers start to wilt and you throw them in the garbage. You keep the memory of that beautiful bouquet. You don't waste your time thinking about how it wilted in the end.

Our relationships with friends, colleagues, partners, and lovers give us joy for years. They may end with angry words and we break the relationship and move on.

We think about the negative parts when we think about our past relationships. We forget the good times; the wonderful evenings, the beautiful dinners, the loving words, the lovemaking, and the children we had.

The only thing we remember is the bad times. We call that relationship a bad decision in our life, or a mistake.

That is not fair to our relationships, past and present.

If we were to judge things according only to how they end, then we would not value life. Any baby who is born is going to end up in a coffin at some point. That does not mean that the beauty of a baby, the laughter, the smiles, or the relationship you had was worthless or a mistake.

So, my friend, even if your relationships end up in a divorce or a broken heart, always remember the good days and cherish them.

THE CENTIPEDE

There was once a centipede. He had many, many legs. He would climb up and down trees happily.

One day, he broke one of his legs. He went through depression and emotional paralysis. "Oh my God! I lost one of my legs. I am not a centipede anymore." He didn't come out of his home in the tree bark for a long time.

One day, the disabled centipede saw a human being running around with only two legs. That made the centipede reevaluate himself. He thought, "If a human can run with two legs, surely I can run with the legs I still have."

When we lose function of a body part, we go through a period of physical and emotional paralysis. If someone loses their eyesight, hearing, or a limb, the person feels paralyzed. When he realizes that blind, deaf, and people without limbs *do* still lead successful and happy lives, he starts accepting his disability.

When people lose wealth, they may consider suicide. Once they realize that before they had all that money they were happy, too, they learn to adjust to an ordinary life again.

Next time you lose something, tell yourself, "I am a centipede. I have a large number of qualities, relationships, and options. Let me see how I can learn to operate again."

THE TOY THAT STANDS BACK UP

Have you ever seen a toy with a heavy, round base and a light top? If you try to make it fall down, it stands back up. It is not possible to make the toy fall down. The toy is made in such a way that it pops right back up again.

Make yourself like this toy. If for whatever reason you feel down, talk yourself back to your upright, positive position. If an inanimate toy can refuse to stay down, shouldn't a living person with a brain be able to figure out a solution to their problem?

Bounce back up just like the toy.

DANDELIONS IN THE BACKYARD

One day, as I stepped into my backyard, I became upset to see many dandelions killing the grass on my beautiful lawn. I brought a dandelion remover and pulled each plant out before they took over the lawn.

Later I saw my neighbor, Joe, working in his front yard. After we greeted each other I asked, "How do you feel about those dandelions?"

He looked at his lawn and said, "They make a good salad. Pluck the leaves and put them in with the rest of your salad. I can't afford to buy them in the supermarket, so I welcome them."

I kept looking at him.

Was he kidding?

No! He was not kidding.

Since that day, before I take the dandelions out, I pluck off the tender leaves for my salad. Joe taught me that every adverse situation in life offers positive opportunities. They are waiting to be plucked up by you.

WILD HORSES

You can enjoy horses if you know how to ride them. You can enjoy the ride as well as the horse. However, if you don't have the skills to ride, you can fall off the horse's back and be trampled under it.

The thoughts in your mind are like horses. Watch them carefully and ride them carefully. You can think logically and take your thoughts to a goal. Look at your thinking like a "thought ride." Your thoughts will help you achieve your goal.

Your wild, uncontrolled thoughts trample you when you worry about the future and berate yourself. You will get agitated, scared, and depressed.

So watch your horses. If they are too wild, let them come and go. Don't ride on them. When you get crazy thoughts, watch them but do not dwell on them. Get busy with something more productive.

Just like you wouldn't ride a wild horse as a beginner, you may refuse to entertain wild thoughts.

THE BAD NEIGHBOR

You have a neighbor who constantly watches you. He makes rude comments about your car and your girlfriend staying overnight. If your grass grows a couple of inches, he calls you a lazy bum. What would you do? You would tell him to shut up. This is your life and you have the right to live it the way you want to.

Now let me ask you; is your conscience cruel like your neighbor? You criticize yourself for having fun, waking up late, forgetting to cut the lawn, or delaying doing your laundry. Is your overly critical attitude making you feel guilty, depressed, and miserable?

You must ask your conscience to shut up so that you can breathe and live your life.

THE BIRD FEEDER

Birds fly to your bird feeder. They are a mix of beautiful, ordinary, and ugly. Sometimes they fight with each other, competing for the seeds. Then they fly away. You watch and relax.

Your thoughts are like the birds. They fly in from nowhere and perch in your mind. Some are beautiful thoughts and others are ugly thoughts. These thoughts compete for your attention. You can let them come and go. Watch them through the window of introspection. Don't react to them, chase them away, or catch them.

Keep your mind relaxed. Imagine yourself as the impartial observer. Sip green tea and watch your thoughts the way you watch the birds. You will smile at the way your mind produces these thoughts, fantasies, dreams, and imaginations.

Stop chasing your thoughts away. There is no need to shoo away the birds. They fly away by themselves.

A FLY IN YOUR CAR

While you were driving one day, a fly entered your car. You tried to hit it with a folded newspaper. All the noise and movement were distracting you from the road. Then you opened the windows of the car and the fly flew out.

We are traveling on the highway of life. Our minds are like the car. Sometimes a repetitive thought enters our minds and starts distracting us like a pesky fly in the car.

The more we try to get them out of our minds, the more they bother us. The less attention you give to these thoughts and the more attention to give to where you're going, the less dangerous life will be for you.

The activities you enjoy are like the windows of the car. They let the useless thoughts fly out and leave you in peace.

Do not react to every thought you have by getting involved in it. You participate in some and observe others.

Sometimes you will have an absurd, immoral, or outright abhorring thought. Do not waste your energy chasing it. Leave it in your mind. Remain busy in what you are doing. It will fly out by itself.

ARE YOU MARRIED TO YOUR IDEAS?

There is an easy way to make sure that you are not buying any cracked eggs. When an egg cracks, it leaks invisible and is stuck to the carton. Open the carton and gently shift every one of the eggs in its place. If you are able to shift the egg, it is good. If it does not budge, it is cracked and stuck.

We are also like eggs. When we are emotionally stable, it is easy for us to change and shift according to changing life circumstances. When we get old and rigid, we stick to the box of our opinions. We do not budge from our position. Listen to other people with an open mind. Maybe they are saying something beneficial that is contrary to your belief.

If you remain stuck on your opinions, people will soon know that you have finally "cracked" and are stuck in your way of thinking.

DOES CHANGE BOTHER YOU?

Every time things settle down, something new unsettles them. You may stamp your feet, fling your keys in frustration, and pull your hair. "Every time there is a break I find some new problems in my life. When will it stop?"

I can understand your frustration. Life changes can be stressful. However, would you really be happy if time froze everything, good and bad? Life is always changing. Changes may cause us to lose family and friends, but they also bring new relationships.

The next time you find yourself fretting about the latest upheaval in your life, look around. You will notice that change not only brings problems, it also brings solutions. The change of seasons brings winters as well as spring and summer.

Geeta, the Hindu holy book, says, "The only constant in our life is change. Change is the essence of life."

Do not resent change; accept it. Embrace it.

WALKING WITH BLISTERS

We get frustrated with many things; school, our job, our kids, our car, our spouse, our parents, our house, and our friends. Well, the lucky ones have these problems.

A wino lying by a street does not have problems with his car because he has no car. He does not argue with his wife because he has no wife. His house does not need a new roof because he does not own a house.

When we focus our attention on problems, we deny the fact that we are lucky to have that part of life.

Maybe it is nature's way of reminding us that we are blessed, just like a blister on our foot reminds us that prior to this time we have been lucky to walk without any pain.

IF YOU WANT THE WATER OUT, FILL THE CUP WITH PEBBLES

Your mind is like a cup. It is full of random thoughts like fears of the future and guilt about unfinished work. They crisscross your mind, making you tense, anxious, and worried.

Drop pebbles of songs, prayers, and work thoughts in the cup of your mind. They will replace your bothersome thoughts. With every positive pebble you drop into your mind, less of the negative will fit into the cup.

A COOL LAKE

If the water in a lake is cool, clean, and refreshing, you will come out feeling refreshed. You will go there repeatedly.

If the water is dirty, you will come out feeling dirty and smelly. You will refuse to go into it again.

The company of our friends and relatives is also like a cool lake. Each time we meet a group of people we like, we come back refreshed and rejuvenated. Make sure you go there.

However, if you feel unhappy, inferior, abused, and angry with a person or group of people, you must ask yourself, "Why am I socializing with these people?"

WHAT KIND OF MEMORIES?

Many of us have unpleasant memories. Our parents, older siblings, or teachers yelled at us. We remember with distaste all those who hit us or shoved us. On the other hand, we smile when we think of those who praised us, cared about us, rewarded us, took us fun places, and loved us.

Take a moment and think about what kind memories you are creating for the children around you. How will they remember you when they grow up? What will they say about you when they talk to their friends?

THE CUSHIONED STICKERS

An expensive figurine can make scratch marks on a table. We put cushioned stickers under it to protect the surface of the table from scratches.

People in power throw their weight around and make others feel resentful. They become insensitive to others' vulnerability. After a while, people avoid contact with them.

When such a person begins to develop better manners such as saying please and thank you, people start to accept them again.

Your money and looks may make you the expensive figurine, but you need a cushioned sticker of manners to protect the surface of people's hearts.

YOU WILL FIND WHAT YOU ARE LOOKING FOR

Let's conduct an experiment. Predict that you are going to find a penny lying in the parking lot. Keep walking with your eyes fixed on the ground. Eventually, you will find a penny.

Now predict that on your morning walk you will find an empty cigarette box on the ground. Keep walking and looking... there! You have found it!

You will find what you are looking for.

Expand this concept into predictions for success and failure in your life. Whatever you predict, you will find in the path of your life.

Predict something good and start looking for and working towards it; you will find it.

ENJOY IT WHILE IT LASTS

People worry about the transitory nature of relationships. They live under constant fear of loss, separation, and abandonment. The fear of the future makes them overprotective, overly attached, jealous, and controlling. Not only can they not enjoy the relationship, they start a negative process of jealousy, anger, and resentment in others that results in a break up.

You see a beautiful rose blossoming on a bush. You stop and gaze at its beauty. You bend down to smell it. How fragrant and pleasant it is!

You do not think, "That rose is going to die in a few days. Why stop to smell it?"

Think of your relationships as rose blossoms. Enjoy them from every angle. You will remember the memory of the fragrance. If a relationship ends, you enjoyed it while it lasted.

So do not worry how a relationship might end. Enjoy it while it lasts.

SAW A SNAKE! IS THAT A PROBLEM?

Make believe that a snake appears in front of you! What will be your response? If you are like me, you will scream and climb on top of a desk.

That is not everyone's response.

If you were a Chinese village farmer and saw that snake, you would have a different response. Your face would light up. You would think that you had an entrée for your dinner. You would picture the beaming smile on your wife's face when she sees the delicacy.

A reptile scientist would be fascinated with this specimen. He would think of publishing the sighting in the Journal of the Society of Reptiles.

The face of a snake charmer from India would light up. Every snake is money for him. He would see the green snake as a crisp hundred-rupee currency bill.

You perceive the snake as a problem or a pleasure depending on your background. Similarly, you interpret a life event as pleasure or pain depending on your attitude.

Be aware that the snake charmer, the Chinese villager, and the scientist are ALL your attitudes. They all exist inside you. Your automatic thoughts can bring fear, but your rational mind can call upon coping thoughts.

Talk yourself into seeing the situation from a different angle. Rather than respond with fear, you can see the situation as an opportunity. Talk to yourself to change your attitude and behavior.

THE MOTHER MEAL OF ALL

My wife believes in the saying, "The family which eats together stays together." Hence, rain or shine, we have family dinner together. She works hard and cooks well.

My friend belongs to a religious group. Many families gathered on a Sunday evening in his house and sang devotional songs for two hours. Then they had a meal together.

I was hungry. They served us with rice, vegetables, and daal. The dinner was poorly spiced and tasteless. I could barely eat in spite of being very hungry.

I don't characterize that day of the tasteless dinner as a bad day. I always call it the mother meal of all. It brought extra appreciation of all the dinners I have eaten at my home since then. I realized how good and delicious the food at my home was.

Sometimes a bad experience can change your life for the better by giving you a fresh perspective.

LET THE SNOW MELT

You looked in your backyard and saw only snow and ice. Everywhere it was white, cold, and frozen. One day, the sun began to warm the backyard and the snow melted. Daffodils and tulips sprang up.

They were all there under the superficial layer of soil. With warmth they all grew and blossomed.

Anger, resentment, insecurity, and fear of rejection are like snow and ice. Your fear of rejection makes you see only negative motives in others.

When you open yourself for friendship, the fear of rejection begins to melt. Your tenderness, love, affection, and caring traits blossom again. You feel surprised. You thought you had no feelings left in you.

All of these feelings were always there; they never went away. They remained dormant inside, waiting to blossom again—and they did.

Never close yourself up. Let people come and go through your life without fear. You never know who will bring a spring in the winter of your life.

NO ONE IS PERFECT

Do not break relationships with others because they have defects. You do not like your mother-in-law because she is too pushy. Your own mother is very critical and demanding of your time. Your sister-in-law is crazy. Your friend leans on you too much. Your boss is unappreciative. Your husband is lost in himself.

The more faults you find in people, the more you lose the positive feelings you have for them. As time passes by, you lose most of your affection for the people around you.

Perhaps you do not perceive yourself to be a perfectionist but that is what you have become. You cannot tolerate faults in others. With time, you lose your affection for them and feel alone in your life.

We are all human beings and not one of us is perfect!

A BUD

A bud opens and blossoms but a blossom crumbles when you try to close it. This is a popular saying in India. It depicts the increasing habits of need, want, and greed.

Once we get used to a big house, expensive car, vacations, spending, and luxury, it is very difficult to scale them down. If circumstances change and you have to do with less, you feel cheated and unhappy.

Keep a watch on your spiraling desires and spending habits, because circumstances always change.

CAUSE & EFFECT

Each time you carry out an action that your heart tells you is wrong, you will get bad results. Think before you do or say something nasty to someone. It will come back to haunt you eventually.

If you spit at the sky, it will fall back on your face. If you do not believe me, try spitting upwards. You will get an unpleasant surprise and be convinced quickly.

LIFE IS NOT A DEAD END ROAD

You are driving to your office. Suddenly you find yourself on a dead end street. What do you do at that time?

You turn around, get off of the dead end street, and find another way to get to your office.

Life is a journey. Your destination is achievement of your full potential. There will be many dead end jobs, broken friendships, failed business ventures, and botched efforts. These dead end roads should not mark the end of your journey. Evaluate the small value of these dead end roads as compared to life's journey. Back track and make new friends, find new relationships, look for different jobs and a new approach to tackle your life.

Dead end roads are not the same as a dead end journey.

WHAT-IF-IT IS

What-if-itis is the disease of the worrywart. He worries, "What if this happens… what if that happens." He conjures up situations and the "what ifs" of life. He makes sense out of nonsense and frets about future.

The answer to the disease of what-if-itis is a pill called "so what."

If you get a thought, "What if our house burns down?" say, "So what, we have insurance." If you get a thought, "What if I have an accident and the car is damaged?" Say, "So what, accidents happen. I know what to do if an accident happens."

Every time you have a bout of What-if-itis, take a "So What" pill.

THE INGROWN TOENAIL

Kathy started spending so much time on introspection that she became hypercritical of herself. She undermined whatever she did. She put herself down and became visibly dissatisfied. She dug in and damaged herself by repeated self-criticism.

Our nails protect and preserve our toes. Sometimes the nails start growing down instead of outwards. They dig into the flesh, causing pain and infection. A podiatrist will remove the excess toenail to give you relief.

Introspection is the toenail of our psyche. It helps us to be aware of ourselves and take responsibility for ourselves and our actions. Thus, it improves our attitude towards others.

Kathy's mindset, however, had become a painful ingrown toenail. Excessive self-criticism had caused the depression. Reducing introspection by focusing outside on the activities of life redirected her energies. It saved her psyche from destruction and depression.

Watch out. If your self-critical toenail is digging into the flesh of your psyche, clip it. Start focusing on the joys of your life again.

WALK AWAY CLEAN

Hurtful and unpleasant events happen to all of us. Some of us experience the hurt and move on. After using the restroom, using toilet paper and washing and drying your hands is the right way to live.

Others live with lingering nasty memories. They tell their woes to sympathetic friends. Listening to their complaints can become unpleasant. They also stink up others' lives with their irritated attitude and remarks.

If someone lived life without using toilet paper, he would stink up his life as well as others'. Therefore, if something bad happens to you, I am sorry it happened.

Use thought toilet paper: remember that shit happens and walk away clean. Do not carry that nasty attitude with you everywhere.

KEEP THE WINDOWS UP ON A DIRT ROAD

Have you ever traveled on a dirt road when a car drove by and spattered dirt on your car? Your windows were up so the dirt fell only on the outside. You continued to drive, unperturbed, untouched, unspoiled, and undistracted from the music on your radio. The closed windows minimized an emotional upset. You thought that the dirt on the outside of your car was inconsequential as far you journey was concerned.

Carry on the journey of life like that. You are driving towards your goal of making a happy life. People say things to you or about you that can be upsetting. It is as if somebody threw dirt on your car. Keep your mindset, keep your emotional windows up, and protect yourself from the consequences of those hurtful words. Keep saying that those words are like the dirt on the outside of your life's car and are minimally important.

Continue on your journey. Focus on the music of your everyday achievements.

YOU CANNOT SEE COLORS IN THE DARK

Have you ever gone into a dark room? You could not see any colors. Everything was black. You switched on the light and the same dark room became full of colors.

Negative thoughts, feelings of inferiority, and absolute negative predictions are the darkness of life. They hide the good things: blessings, opportunities, and hope.

Recognize the state of your inner thoughts. Become aware of when you're focusing on the negative and developing negative thought patterns. It may turn on the light of hope in the dark room of your mind and can make you see all the positive colors you have in life. The darkness was only hiding your colorful room.

Say it aloud, "Right now I am focusing on the negatives. There are many positive things in my life." This will suddenly turn on the light in the dark room of your mind. It will make you see the positives you have. Beginning from a place of gratitude will turn on the light in your mind.

DEPRESSION IS A VALLEY, NOT A WELL

An individual has fallen into a well. The well has no steps and the walls are steep, making it impossible to get out. Ultimately, the individual starts fearing death.

On the other hand, a valley has mountainsides. Someone who has fallen into a valley can slowly inch their way up the slopes, holding on to little projections of rocks, limbs of trees, and plants.

In the midst of depression, we think that we are in a dark well and that we will never get out of it. Remember: "I am not in a well. I am in a valley. Little things that I can do will help me to crawl out of the valley of depression."

Start with small things, like taking a shower, having your breakfast or lunch, or going for a walk. These small routines are the very first small steps that will help you climb out of the valley of depression. Going to your doctor or therapist and taking your medication are the rocks projecting out of the hill that you grab onto to go one step further until you are totally out of the depression.

YOU CAN DROWN IN YOUR BATHTUB

A surfer remains above the waves in the sea. He deals with every one of the waves one at a time. On the contrary, I have heard people slip and drown in their bathtub.

Even small problems can give you a nervous breakdown. You may drown in a small problem like what someone said about you. You may drown in your own negative thoughts.

When dealing with problems one at a time, you can smile knowing that life is challenging and testing you.

Be the surfer on the sea of life and tackle the waves of problems one at a time.

A LUCKY MINDSET

There are many places in a house; the choice is yours as to where you want to spend the most time. You can spend all day in the family room with sunshine or you can spend all your time in a dark, damp closet with the trash.

When we think of good times, good people, and activities that give us pleasure, we create a mental family room full of sunshine.

On the other hand, we can think of all the past hurts and future fears and create a mental trash closet, where we can spend all our time making ourselves miserable.

There's no such thing as being cursed with bad luck or *having* bad luck. There is only a difference in mindset; those who seem to live effortlessly and have good luck are those whose thoughts live in their happy mental family room. Those who feel cursed and like they have bad luck are the ones whose thoughts and perceptions live in the mental trash closet.

WHEN TO BRING AN UMBRELLA

In case it rains, an umbrella will give you protection and you will not get wet.

Nevertheless, permanently keeping an umbrella over your head does not prevent the rain from falling. The umbrella only prevents you from getting wet: it does not stop the rain.

I am using the metaphor of an umbrella for the steps we take to deal with a problem. These actions can take care of consequences of events but they cannot stop the events from happening.

Knowing that difference can help you in deciding whether to take precautionary steps or not.

EVERYONE HAS PROBLEMS

There are no people without wax in their ears. It is universal for an ear to have wax. Whether the person is good-looking or ugly, he has earwax.

Just like wax in our ears, everyone has problems. Sometimes when you get overwhelmed with your problems, you look around and see people smiling, playing, and happy. You start believing that they have no problems.

All of us have problems. It is not possible for people *not* to have problems. Anyone who has money will have money problems: anyone who owns a car will have car problems.

Don't make believe that there are ears without wax in them.

Consideration for Others

IS YOUR SUGGESTION AN ORDER?

People say, "I want to give you a suggestion!" However, sometimes what follows is different. Even if it was a sincere suggestion, the unsaid message is, "If you do not carry out my suggestion, you will be sorry. I will make your life hell. If you use your own brain and come out right, I will stay quiet. If you are wrong, I will remind you forever. I will often say, 'I told you so.'"

The next time you give or receive advice or a suggestion, keep in mind that it is not an order.

EVERYONE IS IMPORTANT

What is more important in the running of a car? Is it the transmission? The lug nuts keeping your tires attached? The answer is both. You cannot run a car with a great transmission and no wheels. Likewise, you can't drive a car with wheels and no transmission. The parts all work together.

We value people according to the jobs they do. We build up a prejudice toward people whose jobs are menial and less glamorous in an organization. We do not give them the recognition they deserve.

Think of what happens if the garbage men go on strike. In a town reeking with stench, they become more important than CEO's, company leaders, senators, and the president.

Everyone in our society is important. They do their own important tasks. It is necessary to recognize the contribution of every person in a family, business, organization, and society as a whole. This ensures that all of the pieces continue working together to form a functioning whole like a family or a company.

The transmission and the lug nuts are important; likewise, the town mayor and the garbage men are important.

DON'T NEGLECT YOUR RELATIONSHIPS

You may neglect important areas of your life if you get intensely involved in one area. You may alienate your family and friends when you start a venture business, a hobby, or a relationship. Later, when you need them, they are not there anymore.

When professional hikers go into a jungle, they let people know where they are going and when they will be back. If they don't return in time, a search team is sent for them.

Even though you are engrossed in your new business day and night, keep in touch with the base camp of friends and family. If you are in trouble, they will be able to help you.

HONK, HONK

To warn other motorists that something is wrong with your car, honk your horn to communicate. They may be able to take actions to save themselves.

In life, if you are in a bad mood, have PMS, are hungry, angry, or irritable, warn other people that you are in a nasty mood today. The other person can take actions to decrease the damage. He may keep a distance, walk away, or make you more comfortable instead of retaliating with nastiness.

When in a bad mood, honk, honk!

HARMLESS SNAKE

A snake in a basket is harmless. Only after it crawls out does it bite and become dangerous.

Evil words in the mind are like a snake in a basket; they are harmless. Once spoken, they bite.

Think twice before you turn your thoughts into spoken words.

TUB OF BUTTER

A spoon makes scraping sounds when you try to get butter out of an empty tub. If the tub is full, you spoon out the butter without any noise.

You will be disappointed if you ask for help from a stressed out or "empty" person. Jack is usually very helpful. He is an accountant. He is the worst person to ask for help when he is busy in the tax season.

Look into the tub of butter before putting the spoon in.

Ask yourself: Is it the right time, the right person, and the right circumstance to ask for help? Ask the other person if you do not know. Reduce your expectations according to the circumstances.

JUDGING BY APPEARANCE

Imagine that you have never seen an orange before. You bite it as you would bite an apple. The peel of an orange is very bitter. Therefore, you declare that it is inedible and never go for it again.

If you are patient and work on passing that peel, you can enjoy the orange.

Some people make opinions about people quickly and turn themselves off. They lose an opportunity to know how wonderful that person is.

Take time and work hard to know them before you make judgments.

EMOTIONAL FLU

Everyone gets the stomach flu at some point but we do not consciously think about that part of life about others. Then one day, someone has an accident in front of us and the whole experience is very displeasing.

Similarly, all of us have problems with family, jobs, money, and work. We should keep these problems to ourselves or talk privately to a small, select group of trusted people. This way we do not affect our social image and the health of others.

Some people talk about their day-to-day problems to anyone who happens to be in their proximity. They do not realize that the listener walks away disliking the complainer. I call this having an "emotional flu" in front of others. You are using everyone like a bucket for your problems.

Be very selective when you complain about having a bad day. Don't subject others to your emotional flu.

DON'T OVER-SHARPEN AND CUT YOURSELF

Have you ever noticed that a blunt knife is useless in the kitchen? It does not cut meat and vegetables well and you have to put force in to get the job done.

Now you take the knife to a sharpener. Voila! It sharpens with three or four strokes. It cuts the vegetables well. You get carried away and sharpen it more. After a few minutes, you are holding your bleeding finger because you cut it with the over-sharpened knife.

Sometimes people are unassertive. They do not express their needs or their criticisms. They take a back seat in their own life. They are like the dull knife and are very ineffective.

One day they decide to begin to speak their minds. It feels good. They overdo it and become aggressive instead. Then they proudly say, "I say it like it is," "I do not mince words," "What you see is what you get." They become so self-centered that they do not care about how others feel. Before you know it, they defeat themselves because no one wants to relate to them anymore.

So go ahead and sharpen your knife, but watch out that you do not overdo it and cut yourself.

GOOD FOR ONE, BAD FOR THE OTHER

When I was seven years old, my uncle would put a dab of his shaving brush on my cheek and deposit foam on my face. I would run screaming with excitement, complaining to him that he was bad. Nevertheless, I always looked forward to it.

Later, when I was 19 years old, I caught my seven-year-old cousin by surprise when I put a dab of shaving lather on her face.

For the next hour, she cried inconsolably. She feared that she would grow a beard like a man. No amount of logic and reassurance helped her.

That incident made me realize that we are all different. What is good for one person may be bad for someone else.

Ask about others' likes and dislikes. Let them teach you how to treat them.

DO NOT DEFLATE YOUR TIRES

You get upset when traffic is too slow or your car gives you problems. You get angry. However, if you kick, slash, and deflate your tires in frustration, you are multiplying your problems. Remember! Your car runs on those tires.

Your spouse, colleagues, children, and friends are very important parts of your life. In the complex ecosystem of life, each of them is as important as the tires of your car. If you get angry and frustrated, you come down hard on them. You say some nasty things to them. They cannot function well with a deflated self-esteem, just like flat tires cannot function.

When angry, do not deflate your loved ones. When deflated, they become useless and compound your problems.

Keep on encouraging them so they will share your load and become an asset to your family or organization.

FREE ADVICE

I had an above ground pool in my back yard. No one was using it. It looked ugly. I asked a few neighbors, but no one wanted it when I tried to give it away.

I put an advertisement in a local newspaper. *Above ground pool with equipment worth $3,000 for $400.* Three people came to buy it and I sold it.

What I could not give away for free was sold for $400.

Advice is something similar. If you give it when it is unsolicited, no one wants it. When people ask for it, they accept it with thanks.

Think before you give an unsolicited free suggestion.

DO NOT YELL

If you yell at your boss, he fires you! If you yell at an employee, spouse, or child, you distract them with the volume of your voice. Their tendency is to run. If their bodies do not run, their attention and minds do. They are not able to grasp what you are saying because of how you are saying it.

We do not attack with our bodies anymore. We now use phones, memos, text messages, emails, lawyers, or the police. Nevertheless, our biological reflex of yelling stays with us.

Keep your voice low. The people you are communicating with will be able to listen and understand better.

THE BRAIN IS LIKE A CALCULATOR

When you enter $100 instead of a dollar for a packet of chewing gum in your calculator, it accepts it as a valid entry. It does not correct your error and gives you a wrong result.

Our mind is like a calculator in day-to-day conversation. Mary said to Jack, "You never help me with the house work." Please note that when Mary said to him, "You *never* help," she was thinking about that day.

Jack took the comment just like the calculator. He understood that Mary felt that he was an unhelpful person. He felt angry.

It is important to watch your use of words like never, always, everybody, and nobody. They are absolute words and create misunderstandings. If you mean to say infrequent, do not use the word never. If you mean to say many people, do not use the word everybody.

Remember, the human brain will accept wrong entries, giving you a wrong overall impression.

YES, YOU ARE! NO, I AM NOT!

Jack found his wife very attractive. He would say, "Rita, you are so beautiful." Rita would reply, "I am not. I'm fat and ugly." He would repeat himself, telling her again how beautiful she was, but she repeatedly replied, "You are lying, you don't mean it." This would end up in an argument with one of them screaming and the other one crying.

The problem was that Jack as well as Rita were only seeing their own point of view and negating the other person's. Jack and I discussed it. After that if Rita said, "I look fat and ugly," Jack would reply, "Rita, I know you *feel* ugly. I can understand how you feel about yourself and I cannot change the way you perceive your body. However, I have a different perception of you. I find you very beautiful. I know that you feel you are not attractive and that is your perception. I cannot change your perception, and neither can you change mine. Let's respect each other's perceptions."

After that, Jack and Rita did not argue about it anymore.

I SAY IT AS IT IS

"I do not take crap from people. I tell it like it is. If you cannot take the heat, stay out of the kitchen. I tell them to shut up. I put people in their place. I speak plain. What is in my heart is what is on my lips. I am not afraid to speak my mind. I call a spade a spade. If someone is out of line, I tell him off. They deserve it."

All of us have known people who say the above. They humiliate other people if they feel that others are different or they "deserve it." They abuse telephone operators, receptionists, the help desk people, and friends and family. They feel that their "ability" to put others in their place is a talent that they possess.

Hanging up on someone has immediate negative consequences. No one wants to associate with foul-mouthed people. They rip apart a teenager staffing a customer service desk. It is embarrassing to be with a foul-mouthed bully.

The truth is that these people lack basic interpersonal skills.

The difficulty lies in protecting people. It takes restraint to remain calm and polite. It takes hard work and interpersonal skills to remain civil in difficult and frustrating situations.

They say you can catch more flies with honey than with vinegar.

Sweet and kind words are effective like honey. They have healing power but they take a lot of restraint and hard work.

DON'T YELL OUT OF WORRY

Think of a time that someone yelled at you. Did you enjoy it? Of course not!

It was 9:00 PM and your wife was not home. You were very worried. You called her cell phone repeatedly; there was no response. You called everyone who could give some idea about her whereabouts; no results. You worried that she was injured, assaulted, or killed. As soon as she walked in, you yelled, "Where have you been? I've been calling everywhere!"

The result will not be a smiling wife who feels cherished.

The result will be a crying wife who thinks she is married to an insensitive cave dweller. She had a flat tire, a dead cell phone, and no cash on her to give to a towing service. She almost froze in the cold. As soon as she arrived, you yelled.

Please do not yell at others. Even if your motive is good, they will perceive yelling as an act of hostility.

DO NOT USE THE BULLETS

As long as the bullets are in your pocket, other people are safe. If others are safe, you are safe as well. If you decide to fire the bullets, someone gets hurt. You end up in a jail.

Just like bullets, words are weapons. The words in your mind are like the bullets in your pocket. They cannot hurt anyone and there is no retaliation. Once you speak the words aloud, the bullet has left the gun and can hurt the feelings of others.

It is okay to have bullets in your pocket or unkind opinions in your head. However, once you fire them at someone, you can do damage. Eventually, they will stay away to stay out of your line of fire.

Think about it before you speak negative opinions. You may end up hurting yourself.

DO NOT STEP ON TOES

A woman may want to dance with you but not be stepped on.

It is hurtful.

A person may want to chat with you but not be made fun of.

It is hurtful.

RAZOR SHARP

It is good to have a sharp kitchen knife to cut vegetables and meat. Nevertheless, if the knife is too sharp, it results in accidental injuries. You it put away in the drawer and seldom use it.

Being assertive is good. You can express your desires, wants, needs, hurts, praises, and feelings to others without discomfort and fear. However, if you communicate your needs in an aggressive and inappropriate way without caring that you are hurting others, people will avoid you. They will call you an overbearing, aggressive, and bossy person.

So make sure that you are assertive but always keep in touch with others' needs.

WHERE ARE THE THORNS?

Jack loves Mary. He gives her a dozen red roses on her birthday. He makes sure to shave off the thorns to protect her delicate hands.

Jack praised his wife to his family, "Mary keeps the house clean, but it's almost too clean." He gave a complement but added "but" in the sentence.

Mary felt hurt that he had given her a complement, a rose, but also a dig about being "too clean," a thorn sticking to the stem.

When you give a complement, make sure it is a pure one without a "but" attached to it.

IT WILL TASTE BETTER TOMORROW

My wife is a great cook. Her cooking is delicious and plentiful. The leftover meats and vegetables marinate overnight and taste better the next day.

People are also like meats and vegetables. The suggestions and advice you give them are like the spices you sprinkle on them. Say what you think and leave them with the idea. Do not insist on an immediate acceptance and agreement. Give them all the information, advantages, and disadvantages of your idea. Now, let them marinate overnight.

Ask them the next day what they feel about your idea. It will taste better then.

THE KNOCK OUT

Boxers wear gloves to avoid hurting their opponents too badly. They don't kill an opponent to announce a victory. Instead, the boxer earns victory by using legal fight moves and knocking out the opponent. These gloves are like a layer of tact standing between the boxers actually killing each other.

Similarly, it takes sensitivity, command of the language, and finesse to criticize with positive consequences. Those people who "say it straight" are often lacking interpersonal skills.

These types of people say rude, hurtful, discouraging, and degrading words. Their words quash others' morale, weaken team spirit, and rupture relationships. People dislike them, evade them, and make fun of them behind their backs. The socially inept stagnate in an organization. If they do progress, they fail to reach their full potential.

Say exactly what you want to say with finesse and sensitivity to others' feelings. The recipient will walk away thankful and enlightened.

SUGARCOATING

No one wants to swallow a bitter pill if a nice-tasting one is available. Therefore, sugarcoating will make it easy to swallow and hence make it effective. Pharmaceutical companies spend millions of dollars to coat their pills.

Sugarcoating is perfectly fine as long as the inner substance is pure. When you are giving someone feedback, start with a genuine, positive comment. Praise a past or recent achievement. Praise a strength and then point out the criticism in a level voice. Suggest a possible solution. Ask how the other person feels about your feedback.

Sugarcoat your words without contaminating the message you want to convey.

NEED TO ARGUE

Once there was a pig. It grew up with its family in a pigsty. The pig did not like the sight or the smell of the mud. It always wished it could live in a cleaner environment like swans and peacocks.

One day it got its chance. A little boy bought it as a pet. The boy was fond of it and got it a clean bed. He allowed it to walk on a clean floor. The pig had gotten so used to the filthy pigsty that it did not enjoy the newfound freedom from filth. Whenever it rained outside and it was muddy, the pig would run out, roll in the mud, and get dirty.

The same happens to us. Joe grew up in a household where his parents argued and abused each other. Joe disliked it but he learned to argue.

He got married to Jane, who is a very loving wife. However, Joe finds reasons to get offended and have arguments. Jane cannot understand his argumentative behavior. In spite of Jane's best efforts, Joe finds reasons to quarrel.

Joe is like the pig that needs to jump into the mud even when a clean environment is available. Joe needs to become aware of his argumentative habits. He needs to recognize that his argumentative behavior served a purpose in his original argumentative family. He does not need it with Jane.

DO NOT LET THE WATER EVAPORATE

If you keep a bottle cap open, the water will evaporate. If you want the water to stay in, keep the bottle cap tightly closed.

That is exactly what happens to your inner secrets. If you keep your lips sealed, they stay in your heart for years. You get restless and tell it to a friend. You instruct him not to tell anyone else. Everyone knows it two weeks later.

If you cannot keep your own secret, what makes you think your friend will?

If you don't want anyone to know your secret, don't open your month. As soon as you open your mouth, it will evaporate to everyone.

XYZ (EXAMINE YOUR ZIPPER)

It is normal to experience anger and to express it in private. However, exhibiting anger in public is a no-no. If you walk around with a chip on your shoulder, you are inviting trouble.

People don't tolerate an irritable and angry person. You will start losing friends and well-wishers. Anger and irritability begets anger and irritability. You may have been special to your mother, but for everyone else you are just another person. No one wants to witness your temper tantrums. Keep your anger covered with civil behavior.

Do not walk around with an open zipper. Police will arrest you! So zip your fly and keep your anger covered.

ONE-WAY STREET

If every car coming from the opposite direction shows you a finger, consider that you may be traveling in the wrong direction on a one-way street. Consider a U-turn.

If more than one person independently points to a certain behavior you have, examine it carefully. Ask yourself, "Why is everyone so critical of this one behavior?"

There is a Spanish proverb: If one person calls you a horse, ignore it. If ten people call you a horse, buy a saddle for yourself.

Reexamine your actions that are bringing unfavorable reactions from others.

THE RIGHT AMOUNT OF SUGAR

Let's say you made a cup of tea for me. You accidentally forgot the sugar. I told you there was no sugar and you promptly put one spoon of sugar into my tea. It tasted great. If you had put two spoonfuls of sugar, I would have felt nauseous.

Apology is like sugar in a relationship. When you have made a mistake, hurt someone, or acted insensitively, then an apology can heal. If you delay apologizing, you can prolong the strife. Conversely, if you apologize all the time for anything and everything, your apology loses its value. Others will see you as spineless, unassertive, and a pain in the neck.

The right measure of apology and forgiveness makes you a person of higher stature.

EXPLOSIONS

Large cities have bomb squads. If they find a suspicious package, the police detonate the bomb in a specially made bunker. The explosion of the bomb does not do any damage outside of that bunker.

Jack had a habit of losing his temper and exploding at his mom, dad, and girlfriend. Teachers asked him to leave because of his nasty outbursts in class. His girlfriend left him after failing to calm his anger.

During psychotherapy, he learned to accept that he had bombs of anger inside. He learned that when he felt the anger-bomb ticking inside of him, he should act like the bomb squad and whisk the bomb away. When angry, he excused himself to go to the bathroom, go for a walk, go work out, or go for a jog. During that time, he calmed down or yelled in the privacy of his room.

Because he has not exploded with anger at his loved ones, he did not need to apologize anymore. His girlfriend went back to him and his parents commended his self-control.

The next time you feel like yelling at your dear ones, take the anger-bomb somewhere it can detonate safely.

EMOTIONAL OUTLET

When you are angry it affects everyone in your vicinity.

Whether or not it hits the intended person, you stay in a bad mood for the rest of the day.

Your anger also hurts *you*. If you are yelling at one employee, other employees resent you. Your anger may do the intended job short-term but it also gives you irritation, resentment, and unhappiness. You are going to carry that with you all day.

Find a way of getting rid of your emotional junk by developing an emotional outlet that allows you to get it away from yourself. I mean, find ways to resolve your anger through hobbies, exercise, or discussions with a confidant or a therapist.

Marriage & Romantic Relationships

AVALANCHE

A small snowdrift dislodges and begins to fall down the slope of a mountain. This can quickly form the nucleus of an avalanche. The more it rolls down, the more snow it gathers and the bigger it gets. As it enlarges, the mass becomes so powerful that it is like a planet rolling down the mountain. Whatever and whoever gets in its way is destroyed.

Two people can also start an immense argument from one accidental comment sliding out of control. This becomes the nucleus of unhappy arguments.

A tired wife wants to enjoy the weekend while the husband wants to finish some work. The wife gets very frustrated and says, "You're very distant." The husband says, "You're very intrusive. Why do you have to continue to intrude on my small amount of free time?"

The words "distant" and "intrusive" become the snowdrift that starts the avalanche. The wife isn't being intrusive; she wanted to have a little fun and relaxation on the weekend. The husband isn't distant, either; he wanted to catch up on his work that had been stressing him out all week.

The husband and wife have to recognize that using certain words like distant, intrusive, and selfish can become the nucleus around which very big arguments can form. Instead, she should say, "I want to go and see a movie today." Her husband should say, "Let me get a little work done first; I will be ready in two hours." There are no harsh words to become an avalanche of an argument.

Watch out for small snowdrifts to prevent an argument from going out of control.

QUALITY TIME

Jill and Jack were a loving couple. Over time, Jack became physically and emotionally abusive. It resulted in separation.

Both miss each other's good aspects and want to come back together but both are scared of failure.

I suggested to Jill this analogy: *Even if a person has loans, it is good to start a savings account.* The more the habit of saving grows, the better the future economic health of that person will be.

I suggested to Jill that she should approach Jack with the idea that they begin spending small blocks of quality time together.

It is okay to save in your savings account even when you are in debt. It is okay to spend quality time together even if there are marital problems between the partners.

The fun time gives the partners incentive to continue to negotiate and forgive each other.

CARS & SPOUSES

Changing cars does not make you a better driver, just as changing spouses does not make you a better spouse.

Instead of changing everything around you, it may be time to take a look inward and see what you can learn and change to make the situations better.

You have to learn to drive better. You have to learn to get along better.

IDEAL HUSBAND

Jackie complains about her unhappy marriage. She says that her husband could spend more time with her, could be sweeter, and could be more tender and sensual towards her. He had promised to slow down at work, but he has not. She feels that he should care more about her, spend more time with their children, and be the husband he could be.

The facts she does not state are that her husband is a very successful man. He has given her anything she and the children have needed. He has been a wonderful father to his children. He has shown appreciation to her for the contributions she has made to the family. He has been friendly and sincere toward her side of the family.

She has gotten so preoccupied with her "could be's" and "should be's" that she has not been able to enjoy what *is*. Time will pass by until what he *is* will be no more.

She will have spent the prime of her life wishing for the "could be/should be" husband, unable to see how great a man he already is. Adopt an attitude of gratitude—your ideal husband could be right before your eyes.

CULTIVATE A PLANT

Let's say that you put a plant on the windowsill in your home and forget about it. In few days' time it will wilt and die and you have to throw it away. On the other hand, if you give it proper sunlight, shade, and water, it will give you beautiful blossoms.

You marry a beautiful woman, bring her home, and leave her totally unattended, neglected, and bored. She is sure to die like that plant on the windowsill. Her body may be alive but her spirits will be dead. That sexy, beautiful young girl will turn into a spiritless, tired, unattractive stranger.

Cultivate a wife, just as you would cultivate a plant.

THE BEST GIFT

I love my wife and am always thinking of ways to please her. She is a quiet person who does not tell me what will make her happy. Occasionally, when both of us are watching TV, I start playing with my toenails and drop them behind the sofa. She watches me do it and says, "Please do not do that."

I told her I would not do it. Nevertheless, it happened repeatedly.

One day I thought of giving her a gift. I decided to give her the gift of quitting my annoying habit. To do that, I have started using a nail cutter weekly in the privacy of my bathroom.

Think about an annoying habit you have and quit it as a gift for someone you love.

JUNK CAR

Is your car a junk car? You spent a lot of money trying to fix it. Due to this junk car, you have been late to your job and stood on the highway during winter. It is time to throw away that junk car. Don't hesitate because it was a good car at one time.

If you are on a highway, maybe it is time to move on and leave it on the side of the road. You can still cover more distance walking, hitchhiking, renting a car, or using the train or bus than you can trying to fix your car.

As a couple, you have irreconcilable differences like cruelty and physical abuse. If you have already gone to marriage counselors repeatedly and failed, move on with your life. The fact that this marriage was a good marriage at one time does not make a difference now. It's time to leave it behind and move on with your life.

OIL CHANGE

Joe bought a new car and was very excited. He loved driving it. Whenever he saw that the gas tank was empty, he filled it up. A few months later, it caught on fire and burned. The car was towed to the garage. The mechanic asked him if he had ever taken his car for servicing and Joe said that he had not. He had been too busy to get the servicing. The mechanic told him that the engine had burnt because of neglect.

You may find the same situation with someone you love. You got into a relationship. You enjoyed being with her. You married her and had children. You went to your office from morning until night. You came home tired and expected a beer while you sat on the sofa in front of the TV.

You were busy earning the livelihood and she carried the load of the household. She felt abused because you leaned on her for all your needs. She became depressed and withdrew. Finally, she gave in. She divorced you. You were surprised and couldn't figure out why she left you and your lifestyle.

You never realized that she burnt out due to your emotional neglect.

The car cannot run on gas only, it needs a change of oil, too. Your marriage needs maintenance, too. Maybe it's time to take a vacation or do something special for her.

THE CACTUS FLOWER

You live in a desert. You go for miles and the only thing that surrounds you is sand. One day, you see a beautiful bloom on a cactus on the roadside. What do you do?

Do you pass by it and continue to complain about the sand, or do you pick up this little cactus with the bloom and bring it home? Let's say you plant it. If you continue to do that, you can have a cactus garden and fill your house with beautiful blooms.

Some individuals do not find anything interesting in their spouse. They complain that their partner is boring, dry, and colorless. They verbalize it and let their spouses know their feelings about them. Married life seems like a desert to them and they feel that they are dying a slow death.

However, Mary found one quality in James that she absolutely loved. His love for his work fascinated her. She not only enjoys it herself, she let him know how much she appreciated it. She ignored all the sand around her. She noted the cactus bloom. She tells her friends and relatives about the positive quality of her husband. By constantly noticing and verbally rewarding her husband, she turned her married life around and James started to become more attentive to her needs.

The blossoms of his kind words and good deeds filled her life in return.

AVOID CROSS-CONTAMINATION

You are carrying three small containers on a tray. One has milk, the second has bleach, and the third one has motor oil. You carry it carefully to avoid splashing. When you arrive, you can use milk for drinking, oil for your engine, and bleach to clean your toilet.

On the other hand, if you are careless, the bleach, milk, and oil splash around and spoil each other. You cannot drink the milk, use the motor oil, or use the bleach.

Let me use this metaphor to explain relationships in our life. If you are angry with your husband for something, you refuse to have sex. It does not solve the problem but splashes tension into your love life. Now you have two problems.

Don't let the day's problems spill into your night. Sit down with him during the day and hash out differences.

THE CHICKEN OR THE EGG

Which came first, the chicken or the egg? This question could be the reason that a husband and wife end up arguing all evening.

On the other hand, another couple begins to discuss the case of, "the chicken or the egg." The wife comes up with the idea of making chicken and egg curry. She looks at her husband with half-closed eyes and says, "You can pick which you would like first, the chicken or the egg." They laugh, beginning a beautiful evening together.

Arguments are universal. It is very important for both partners to recognize the start of an argument. Watch out! Kill the argument before it gathers force.

Don't try to win an argument. Whichever partner kills the argument is the winner.

MOMMY IS MAD

When you were a child, you believed that you ate, used a toilet, and walked around and it made Mommy happy. You also believed that anything wrong you did made her unhappy.

Mom was the center of your world.

As you grew older, you realized that Mom had other reasons to be happy, upset, or worried. You realized that you were important to Mom but you were only a part of her life and not her whole world.

When you got married, you went through the same cycle again. If your wife was unhappy, you became a child again. You thought that she was unhappy because you did something wrong.

If you want to grow up, you do what adults do. Be sensitive to her pain but don't assume that you are the center of her universe. There are many, many more things that could upset her. Keep an open mind. Ask her what is bothering her and listen to what she says.

Remember! She may be smoldering about something other than you but may explode in front of you because you are the only one who listens! Unless you have the objectivity of keeping yourself separate from your wife, you will not be able to find the source of her aggravation and help her.

BANANAS SPOILED

Cynthia was married for 20 years to a successful attorney. The last four years had been hell. She wondered if he was becoming an alcoholic. She pointed out her concerns to him. He laughed at her, became belligerent, and broke things.

He grew more distant from the family. It finally resulted in a divorce.

Cynthia feels abandoned, bitter, angry, and sad. She feels that Jack wasted 20 years of *her* life. She wants to wipe out Jack from her heart, mind, and her children's lives.

I asked her, "Let's say you had twelve bananas and the last four spoiled. Would you like to throw up the first eight bananas by inducing vomiting?" Cynthia said that she would not treat the first eight bananas badly just because the last four bananas spoiled.

She saw the wisdom in the metaphor. She acknowledged that her 16 years of marriage were good and that no one could take them away from her and her children.

She should not retroactively reject 16 good years of married life just because her marriage was breaking up after four extremely difficult years.

HURT THE PERSON BUT NOT THE RELATIONSHIP

Jack is upset about Martha's unfair treatment of him. He has two choices.

He can tell her about the unfair treatment, hurt her feelings, and be at peace with himself. She may feel hurt temporarily but would recover by evening. Their loving relationship will continue.

His second choice is to keep his mouth shut, simmer inside, kill his love for her, and hurt the relationship by collecting resentful feelings.

In the future, when you are in a similar situation, communicate. Go ahead; hurt the person a little but not the relationship.

THE FRIGHTENING MASK

If you put on a scary mask and face a little boy, he will get scared. If you put on smiling mask, he starts laughing. His little mind cannot perceive your face behind the mask. The mask becomes reality for the child.

When your wife gets angry, who does she remind you of? Is it your mom? Is it your father? Is it your brother?

Ask yourself and answer honestly.

Once you know the childhood figure she reminds you of, you will know what mask you are seeing on her face. Now ask yourself how you felt about the childhood figure whose mask you are seeing on her face.

This exercise will give you answers to why you get excessively angry, paralyzed, distant, cold, or scared. You perceive an important childhood figure on the face of your wife. You then start treating her the way you treated the childhood figure.

Beware of the scary masks you put on your wife's face. Can you try to remove the mask from her face and see her as she really is? Once you have done that she will not look so scary.

DON'T BREAK YOUR VASE

Rachel's first marriage to Ron ended because he was busy partying. After six years of marriage, the love died and they divorced. Rachel married Tom.

Tom stopped having sex with Rachel. She asked him what the matter was. He had no answer. With every day, Tom moved further away. She cried, wept, and begged him to go for marriage counseling. Tom did not show any interest.

"What is wrong?" she would ask. He would always say, "Nothing."

Rachel asked for a divorce. She moved out. After one year of divorce, she met Richard. He is intelligent and well-mannered. He says that she is the best thing that happened to him. Their romantic life is rich.

The love of the men was like a bouquet of flowers and her ability to love is like a vase. Each time the bouquet wilted, she filled the vase with fresh flowers.

Keep the vase of your heart carefully. Do not let it break. There will be many bouquets coming your way.

SICK OF YOUR APARTMENT?

You look around at peeling walls, clutter, and old furniture. You feel sad looking at it.

What do you do? You go and discuss with your partner. Buy some paint for the walls, spiff up the curtains, and bring in some comfortable furniture. Now you are happy with your apartment.

Similarly, if you find that your relationship is becoming boring, refurnish it with new ideas, activities, hobbies, vacations, and friendship.

APPLES AND PAIRS

Rita, a widow, complained about her boyfriend: "Why doesn't he talk more? Why isn't he warmer?" She felt angry towards him. She would resist his sexual advances and his suggestions for vacations. She felt irritated by his ways. She retaliated by shouting or withdrawing. Her boyfriend could not understand her erratic behavior.

She constantly compared her new boyfriend to her late husband.

You can bite into an apple but cannot expect it to taste like a pear. Likewise, you cannot bite into a pear and expect it to taste like an apple. They are different fruits.

She was unconsciously comparing her boyfriend with how she remembered her husband. She was used to an apple and could not understand that her boyfriend was a pear.

If she learned to recognize that her boyfriend was different but not defective, she would enjoy him much more.

YOU CAN'T STAND ON THE TIP OF A PYRAMID

It takes two to start arguments. In a marriage, the wife may say something that incites the husband. Instead of thinking, "Well, she's in a bad mood," the husband responds in a curt manner. He comes back with a negative remark. The next morning, instead of saying good morning to him, she says that she made a wrong decision to marry him. They continue to make spiteful remarks. They are adding layers of anger and building a pyramid with it.

With each layer of argument and anger added to the pyramid, their patience grows shorter. Eventually they reach the top, where one partner defeats the other. There is not enough room on the tip of the pyramid for two. The defeated one falls to the ground, hurt, disrespected, and angry.

The person on the top of the pyramid is alone. The sadness and the guilt of having hurt the other person makes him feel like a loser, not a winner. What use is winning when you are alone there, unable to share with your loved one? Stop building layers of anger and resentment before you reach the pinnacle of the pyramid that you are building. It will be very lonely there.

DON'T TRADE IN A CAR BASED ON THE CONDITION OF ITS TIRES

Joe was not getting along with his wife, Rita. She was very disorganized. He divorced Rita to marry Patty. The latter does not have Rita's problems because Joe made sure of it when he was courting her.

You may be sick of the flat tires, but the rest of your car is okay. If you sell your old car and buy another car with newer tires, you may be in for some surprises. Unbeknownst to you, the next car may have costly transmission problems. You will wonder if selling your car was such a good idea. Maybe you should have spent money to buy new tires for your old car?

As the days and months passed by, he recognized that Patty had problems with insecurity and money. She did not spend any of her own money. Instead, she wanted him to spend his money all the time. He discovered that she stole his money, too. This was the start of his unhappiness with Patty.

He remembered that Rita had faults, but he also remembered her trustworthiness. Maybe he should have gone for marriage counseling and worked out his differences with Rita. It would've been like getting new tires for an otherwise great car.

DO NOT SPREAD YOUR GERMS

Jack had an argument with Mary. She said some bad things. Jack left the house and moved in with his mother. He told his mother about Mary and how bad she was.

If you get a cold, do not go around coughing in everyone's face. Eventually you will get better but everyone else will have your cold and will cough right back in your face to re-infect you. You will not want those germs again.

The next morning, Jack's 5-year-old daughter called him to invite him to school parent night. In the evening, as soon as Mary saw Jack, she apologized for being nasty. She told him it was her premenstrual tension, which caught both of them by surprise. She asked him to come home, saying, "The kids miss you so much. I do, too." Jack felt better and eventually went home.

Jack's mother, however, was still very angry. She could not understand why Jack would return to such a nasty woman.

Now Jack and Mary were getting along fine, but Jack had turned his mother against Mary. Every time he talks to his mother, he has to hear negative things about his wife.

He infected his mother with germs of anger and resentment. He is over his anger flu but his mother still has it. Now, he is getting it back.

When you have a problem with your friends or your spouse, let the people around you continue to relate to them on their own merit. They do not have to mirror your relationship.

Do not infect them with your resentment.

WHY DOESN'T SHE DO IT, TOO?

Make believe that you and your spouse are standing in your above ground pool. The right half is your side of the pool and the left half is your partner's side. There are two faucets filling it with water, one on your side and one on her side. There are two drains near the bottom of the pool, one on each side.

Suddenly you both realize that the water level has risen two inches more than you need for a safe swim. There is a possibility of both of you drowning. Your partner yells out to you, "I am drowning here!"

You scream with a solution, "Let the water out by opening up the outlet and shut off your faucet!"

However, your partner does neither. Instead she replies, "Why should I be the one to do it? Why do I always have to open and close the faucets on my side of the pool? Why can't *you* ever be the one to control the water level?"

You insist that because she is the one having trouble, she should take action. The water level continues to rise, and both of you drown.

The negative behaviors of both partners contribute to marital unhappiness just as the positive behaviors bring happiness. It does not matter who adds the water or lets it out—it affects both partners.

You do not want to have to, "give in," "adjust," or, "stoop down." You feel you have done enough already and now it is the other person's turn.

To save your life, take action on your side. It will save you as well as your spouse. Your actions will also give you a sense of control in your life. When your spouse sees you change for the positive, he or she may change.

TAKE CARE OF YOUR SHOES

Imagine two scenarios.

You impulsively bought a pair of tight shoes. However, you expanded and took care of them. With time, the leather began to soften, expand, and mold to your feet. As the time passed by, they became one of your favorite pairs.

The second scenario is that you bought a very expensive and comfortable pair of shoes. You were careless. One day you left them outside on the deck in the rain. Now they wear and look awful.

Your marriage partner is like a pair of shoes, too. You make sure that you take care of her with love. With the passage of time, she becomes a comfortable, conflict-free partner. She understands you and your needs. She fits like a comfortable pair of shoes.

Conversely, you married a beautiful and intelligent woman but treated her with neglect. There was no quality time together. You had no mutually satisfying hobbies. Soon she became a nagging and unhappy wife. The arguments and mutual neglect made you unhappy.

Take care of your shoes and your spouse well. Ask yourself every day: What can I do today to make my partner happier?

Your small deeds to make her happy now will pay off big in the long run.

THREE OVERCOATS AND ONE HOOK

Make believe that you have a coat hook on the wall. It was made to hang one coat. You hang a second coat and the hook starts bending. However, when you try to hang a third coat, all of them fall off and get dirty.

I am talking about our expectations from our friends and family members. The expectations we have are the heavy coats. The hook on the wall is our loved one. Everyone, however strong, has limits of their time, interest, desire, and energy.

When your expectations are more, your spouse can gear up to meet you halfway. If your expectations cross her limits, the hook breaks. You have the choice of accepting the limitation of the hook and hanging only one coat. Use a closet for the rest of the coats.

If your spouse does not have time to take care of your boredom and restlessness, develop other hobbies. Join the YMCA. Join a local biking club.

If you put too much pressure on the hook, it will come off of the wall.

If you have a wife who is unassertive and submissive, watch out! She has limits, too. If you put pressure far beyond her capability and she has no ability to refuse, your marriage ends up in divorce.

It is also possible that she will stay with you but will have a nervous breakdown or turn to food, drugs, or alcohol.

THE STORY OF MISS NUT AND MISTER BOLT

The best factory in the area manufactured a nut and a bolt.

However, when Mr. Bolt tried he could not fit into Ms. Nut. Arguments and blaming ensued. Their arguments always ended in blaming their manufacturers. "The mechanic who made you must be a crazy nut, too!" she would say. Mr. Bolt would reply, "You are where manufacturing got screwed up." They eventually began to feel that they were not made for each other.

However, Ms. Nut had an idea. She suggested they go and see a mechanic. Mr. Bolt hesitated initially, but eventually agreed to go.

They went for rust removal therapy. After a few tries, they were able to fit together. The nut fell in love with the bolt again. They lay together in the toolbox in perfect unison.

Years passed by.

Because of their years of extreme closeness, they fused with each other. After an attempt to unscrew the pair, the mechanic declared that rust bonded them and now they were useless for anyone else.

They again went for rust removal therapy. Both sighed with relief as they learned to tolerate being separate from each other. It felt so free.

People find "perfect" mates. Once they get married, they start having problems with each other's habits. If marital partners recognize the problem and get marriage counseling, they can change or adjust accordingly.

On the other side, togetherness, which excludes other people and activities, may be bad. If a man wants to start singing in a choir, his partner may fear that he will meet someone more interesting than her.

Remember that you may be a perfectly made bolt, but you have to work hard to fit into a perfectly made nut. If there is a problem, get marriage counseling.

THE ZESTY TOMATO SAUCE

Mary was a very good wife. She took care of her family well. When John returned home from work at night, she always served him a hot meal. Even though she was often tired to the point of exhaustion, she would agree to have sex. She did all of the above not because it gave her joy but to prevent her feared consequence: divorce.

After years of bitter arguments, her parents divorced when Mary was 10 years old. She vowed that she would do *everything* to avoid a divorce in her life. When she got married, she avoided all arguments. Many times when John was unjust or outright nasty, Mary kept her outside appearance of happiness. She was so sweet.

If you want to make a zesty tomato sauce, you add tomatoes, vinegar, wine, salt, black pepper, cayenne pepper, oregano, basil, and rosemary. Some chefs tell you a secret ingredient in their sauce: *half a teaspoon of sugar.*

On the other hand, if you make a sauce with *only* the secret ingredient—sugar—you will end up making syrup, not a sauce.

She was so sweet that she became syrup instead of a tangy sauce. Soon John began to lose interest in Mary and felt turned off. He found her dull and boring. There was no spice and no kick.

During marriage counseling sessions, Mary began to recognize that she was overdoing her sweetness. Mary came to realize that this marriage was not her parents' marriage and that fate had not predestined a divorce. She took risks. She began to act spontaneous. She expressed her likes, dislikes, and her love for John. Soon John had his long-lost girlfriend back.

Are you hiding parts of your personality because of fear of some consequence you're convinced will come true? People all have multifaceted personalities; don't be afraid to let yours shine.

CROSSING A RIVER

If a man stands on a boat to cross a river, he can do it with ease and joy. If he tries to cross the river by standing on two boats with one leg on either boat, the man falls in between the boats.

A man is happy in his marriage. He is crossing the river of life well. Then he starts having an affair. All affairs eventually come out. His wife and girlfriend both give him an ultimatum to make his decision. He cannot decide which way to go.

The married man is now standing on two boats and they both begin to move away from him. His emotions, like his legs, are torn apart. He falls in the middle of the river of sadness, guilt, unhappiness, separation, and divorce. His crossing of the river would have been so pleasant on one boat. Why did he choose such an unwise course?

Travel on one boat. Do not cheat on your spouse.

YOU GOT THE HOUSE

Jane and Jack got married after a loving and tender courtship. They moved into a house that they could not afford. Jack started working overtime while Jane accepted a night shift; it paid more. They communicated by leaving notes for each other. Lack of time, different schedules, and exhaustion resulted in fewer contacts and a loss of intimacy.

Jack had an extramarital affair. Jane was considering one. Eventually, the stress got to them and they ended up in divorce.

Whenever you make a decision in your marriage, ask yourself, "How will this affect our relationship in the long run?"

Always keep the relationship your #1 priority.

HOW A FOREST FIRE SPREADS

Green trees are damp from the inside. I am sure you have had an experience with trying to burn a damp log. You cannot start a fire with it. If that is true, how is it that forest fires spread and get out of hand? Well, when the dry brush is burning, the heat of the burning brush starts drying out the green trees. When their moisture is gone, they catch fire. Once the trees start burning, their heat dries up the next grove of green trees. Once dried by the nearby heat, those catch fire, too. That is how the fire spreads.

Do you express your anger in the form of withdrawal, the silent treatment, yelling, cursing, and underhanded reminders about past mistakes? When that happens, you become the burning tree. Your spouse, who has love and tenderness for you, feels the heat of your seething anger. She tries to give you love, apologize, or give you a hug and a kiss to end the argument. A constant, unending anger from you slowly starts killing the tenderness in her heart. She becomes like the dry tree. One day she catches fire, too. She burns and the fire's intensity doubles. It burns all the love, tenderness, joy, and affection between the two of you.

Watch your expressions of anger.

Addiction

THE BOTTLE DROWNS ACCOMPLISHMENTS

Most of the time, getting drunk is harmless fun. However, in many cases, you could wipe out all of the hard work you have already done socially, at home, at work, and towards your health.

Some social drinkers will develop alcoholism. During episodes of binge drinking, the problem drinker will conduct himself in a way that hurts the most important people in his life and drives them away.

Each new episode of problem drinking washes away your achievements like sand castles on the beach. When you are sober, each day is like a brick, raising the castle of your life. If you want to build a sturdy castle and continue making progress, don't wash away your achievements with waves of binge drinking.

SELF-MEDICATING

Patients often tell me that they have been dealing with their depression or anxiety by "self-medicating." By this, they mean that they have been using alcohol, marijuana, or other substances. They often combine these substances with potentially lethal effects.

I tell my patients, "Please do not use the word 'medicating.' You are aggrandizing your drug addiction by calling it 'self-medicating.' You are not medicating yourself; you are poisoning yourself. Medication heals. What you are doing is harmful."

From now on, when you refer to your abuse of marijuana, alcohol, opiates, or cocaine, tell yourself that you are self-poisoning, not self-medicating. Call a spade a spade.

STOP AND CHANGE YOUR DIRECTION

If you get lost, the logical solution is to stop at a gas station and ask for directions. Change your course and rectify your mistake.

If you are fired, in debt, or your relationships are in turmoil, ask yourself, "Am I taking the right highway?" You may realize that you are going in the wrong direction. It could be excessive drinking, gambling, cheating, or spending. Whatever direction you are taking, you may arrive at destinations you never planned for: arrests, DWI, or collection court.

Stop at a "gas station" like AA, NA, GA, a credit bureau, or a friend to find how to get on the right highway so that you can reach a destination of happiness and success.

BE A KID AGAIN

Look at a group of kids playing. They laugh and play without inhibition.

What? You need to have couple of drinks to loosen up, to enjoy, to play, to laugh, and to speak like kids.

What has happened to you?

Go back few years and dig out that spontaneity buried inside you. Then you would not need a drink to enjoy a dance again.

EIGHT JOB INTERVIEWS PER DAY

When you go for a job interview, you go through a stress reaction. Your body produces a rush of adrenaline. Your blood pressure and heart rate go up and your muscles tense up.

Caffeinated drinks produce adrenaline in your body. Each cup of coffee is an equivalent to the stress of a job interview.

Adrenaline gives a mini-stress reaction. However, when people drink eight coffees a day, it causes caffeinism, a chronic stress-like condition. Everyone else can see your impatience, hurry, and irritability.

Now make believe you go to eight interviews daily and it goes on for years. You will remain chronically stressed out and will develop anxiety, irritability, distractibility, and impatience. You will be unable to sit comfortably. You will pace and be unable to rest.

Please reduce your caffeinated drinks. You will reduce the stress levels in your life.

YOU ARE A MATCHBOX

You can keep a matchbox securely and without harm for years. However, one matchstick can light up a wild forest fire.

If you have problems like overeating, drinking, or sexual and drug addiction, you are safe as long as you do not act out. If you do not open the cork of the bottle, it is safe.

If you take one drink, go to a prostitute, or buy one lottery ticket, the fire of the addiction spreads to your whole being and consumes you.

So, watch out for that first drink, first flirtation, first hit, first bet, first binge, and first purchase. Do not light up the matchstick to start a forest fire.

ARE YOU A CANDLE OR A CAN OF GASOLINE?

When you light up a candle, it burns for many hours. It lights up the room for a long time. When you light a match to a can of gasoline, it explodes into a big ball of fire, consuming itself as well as destroying its environment.

Social drinkers are like a candle. When you show them the matchstick, i.e. a drink, they slowly sip it, sometimes leaving some of it in the glass when they leave.

An alcoholic is like a gasoline can which cannot burn slowly. If they start with one drink, they end up finishing the bottle or getting drunk.

You may have been a candle at one time. Maybe now you have turned into a gasoline can of smoking, drinking, taking drugs, or gambling. Whatever your addiction has been, it has changed your nature from that of the wax of the candle to that of the gasoline. Maybe at one time you could do with one drink and walk away. Now you cannot.

Please do not try lighting a match to the gasoline can with one drink. Not only will you endanger your sobriety, but also you may jeopardize the welfare of your loved ones.

GASOLINE IS STILL GASOLINE, EVEN AFTER 10 YEARS

You left a can of gasoline in a corner of your garage 10 years ago. It laid there, safe. Even though the last ten years have been eventless, the liquid in the can has not changed its combustible property. If you show it a flame, it will explode. The longer you keep it away from the flame, the longer you can avoid an explosion.

Similarly, if you had a problem of drinking, drugging, smoking, or gambling in the past but have remained sober for 10 years, you have not changed the addiction itself. If you do your drug of addiction, you are going to explode again. So always remember, sobriety can disappear in a second with one slip.

A heroin addict may take five years to develop a $300 a day habit. He goes to Narcotics Anonymous to kick his habit. After ten years of sobriety if he picks up heroin, it will take him less than a week to get back to his $300 a day habit.

Remember! Once an addict, always an addict. Once a gasoline can, always a gasoline can.

BE AWARE OF THE MUGGER

Muggers tiptoe behind you until they are next to you. They may even walk right up to your face and smile innocently. Once you are within arm's length, they attack you and rob you. Alcohol, cigarettes, gambling, and drugs can be life's muggers.

One day you attend a New Year's party. Someone fills your glass with bubbly without asking you. Everyone raises his or her glass to say, "Happy New Year!" The waiter comes to refill your glass again and you think, "What's the harm?" Then, one day you hear that red wine is good for the heart so you start taking a glass of wine with dinner. This becomes a daily habit. After a while, you start taking two glasses of wine. Soon after that, it becomes three glasses and then the whole bottle. You start having blackouts and forget what happened during your drinking.

One day, the police finds you confused and disoriented. They bring you to a hospital emergency room. Your liver has enlarged. The doctor gives you a diagnosis of cirrhosis of the liver. You are told that you have three more years to live.

You never realized when this friendly alcohol became the mugger of your life. Do not begin a friendship with alcohol, drugs, gambling, or cigarettes lightly. They could be your best friend one moment and turn into a mugger the next.

Connecting with Difficult Patients

HELPING PATIENTS TO OPEN UP

Your patient sits quietly and does not give information.

Doctor: If you were a dentist and I was your patient, could you help me if I refused to open my mouth?

Patient: No.

Doctor: Well, unless you open your mind to me by talking about what's bothering you, I cannot help you.

A FEAR OF SIDE-EFFECTS

When a patient in a psychotic or depressive episode tells me that he does not want to take medicine because of its side effects, I say, "Suppose your house is on fire and a fire engine throws water on your burning house. There will be water damage. Would you stop the fire engine?"

The patient says, "No."

I ask, "Why?"

The patient says, "Because the house will get burnt down."

I say, "The illness is like the fire. It is burning your health down. Let me give you medicine. The medicine may cause side effects like the water damage, but ultimately, it will save your life. Once the illness is under your control, we will manage the side effects."

Patients usually see the wisdom behind this metaphor and accept the medication as a necessary part of their healing.

THE HYPOCHONDRIAC DRIVER

Many years back, I heard a strange and faint noise from the rear of my car. I stopped the car and got out. I looked around but could not find anything wrong. The noise continued, so I took the car to the mechanic. He fixed a few things, nothing specific, charged me $300.00, and declared that everything was okay.

Driving the car home from the dealership, I heard the same noise from the rear of the car. One week later, I took the car in again. After the mechanic looked, checked, and drove the car himself, he gave the car a clean bill of health.

For the next few weeks, whenever I drove I kept hearing that noise. I shut off the radio so that I did not miss that noise. One day I realized that my concern with the well-being of the car was like that of hypochondriac patients. They are so concerned about small variations in their health that most of their time is spent checking their body over and researching various diseases. One patient of mine used to give me the details of the day-to-day variation of the color of his bowel movements. This happened despite his doctors telling him that all his tests were normal.

As soon as I realized that I was behaving like a hypochondriac about my car, things began to change. I said to myself, "My car has been declared healthy. It is not going to explode into little shreds while I am driving down the highway. The noise is a small variation and not a forewarning of a disaster." I turned the radio up. I kept and enjoyed that car for another two years.

Sometimes we tune in to small variations in our physiology, the structure of our face, the shape of our nose, the ears, or the breasts. Sometimes, we start worrying about our house, our finances, or our profession. We develop a hypochondriac obsession. We tune out everything else and put the microscope of our attention on our worries.

WHY IS IT TAKING SO LONG FOR THE DEPRESSION TO LIFT?

We have started treatment in the form of medication and psychotherapy. It takes time to get well.

When you break a leg bone, a doctor puts a cast on your leg. It takes a few weeks for the bone to heal. After the cast is removed, you have to go through physical therapy to strengthen your leg to its pre-fracture level of functioning.

You have had a fracture of emotions: depression. It is going to take time to heal. Instead of the cast we are using medicine, and instead of physical therapy we are using psychotherapy.

So hang in there—we will see the results.

LIMIT YOUR EMOTIONAL TALK

Anxiety, depression, and high emotionality makes a patient talk to many people. Obsessive compulsive, hypochondriac, body dysmorphic, and eating disorder patients constantly talk to everyone in their environment. It feeds their fire.

Limiting talk would limit preoccupation.

This is what I tell them: Treat me as your emotional toilet bowl. Bring all of your crap and dump it in my office. Do not talk to anyone else. Keep your sofa, bed, and living room free of crap.

When you talk about your emotional problem to others, you soil the relationship. Keep it clean. Only use me for that. A toilet bowl is made for that purpose. You flush it and it is clean.

As the patient limits their emotional talk to others, their preoccupation with their own affliction decreases.

I WANT TO STOP TAKING MEDICATION

This is a common feeling for many people who are on medication for chronic illnesses, including Diabetes and high blood pressure. People start seeing medication as a reminder of their illness. If they don't take medicine, they are not reminded of the illness. Slowly they start thinking that the medicine is the problem and if they don't have any medicine they won't have any problems.

They forget that the medicine was given to them because they had an illness. If the medication is thrown in the garbage, they are throwing away the solution. The problem remains.

The disease is the lock. The medicine is the key. By throwing away your key, the lock does not disappear. Now you still have the lock but no keys.

Try to work on your locks without resenting the keys.

ONE PILL WAS VERY HELPFUL; CAN I TAKE MORE?

The room is dark and you can't see anything. Then you switch on a light bulb. You can see everything clearly in the room. Making the light brighter and brighter does not give you more clarity. It makes the room hot, hurts your eyes, and costs more. It does not give additional benefit.

If the medicine helped you and it is the optimum dose, more of it will not give you more benefit.

CAN YOU REDUCE MY DOSE OF MEDICATION?

Sometimes patients want to reduce the dose of their medication. They don't have a rational reason like side-effects, etc.

Doctor: Why do you want 2mg instead of 4mg? You have been well stabilized on 4mg.

Patient: I don't want to take all that medicine!

Doctor: What is your eye glass number?

Patient: it is +3.

Doctor: Next time when you go for an eye checkup, ask the ophthalmologist for +2.

Patient: Why would I do that? I see well with +3.

Doctor: I am suggesting you reduce your eye glass number, just like you want to do with your medication.

Patients who wear eye glasses find it an absurd suggestion and immediately see the logic of not reducing medicine without a good reason.

For those who don't wear glasses, the following conversation works.

Doctor: When you go to buy shoes, get one size smaller. Why wear a larger shoe?

The patient starts smiling and says, "OK. I understand. Give me 4mg."

WELL-KNOWN RECIPES AND THE EXPERT CHEF

Let's say that a patient comes in shopping around for a new doctor. He wants a new medication. He brings a list of multiple medications half-tried for few days each. His expectation is that you will come up with some new miracle med.

You say that a chef cooks good food with common ingredients. He does not need an exotic spice to cook good food. Similarly in treating your illness it is not the new medication which will work but the use of well-tried meds by an expert.

If you fall into the trap of starting new medicines all the time, you become another failed statistic.

We make tasty food with well-tried spices, sugar, salt, flour, and butter or oil. The newer the spice is, the higher the chances are that people may not like it.

I tell them that many patients come to me from their previous doctors with a lack of success. I try the same medication in the right doses and for a long enough period. This way the results can be great.

I tell them that if I came to their kitchen and tried the same ingredient as his mom, I probably will make something nasty, as compared to his mom.

I am a good psychiatry chef. I have been in the "psychiatry kitchen" for the last 40 years. I know my ingredients and I know my recipes.

I am an expert in the medicines I have tried for years. Please give me a chance to try familiar ingredients and recipes. If those don't work when properly dosed and taken, we will try other ones.

HOPEFUL TO HOPELESS

During the throes of a depressive episode, a patient comes in feeling hopeless and useless.

I describe what the illness of depression is.

I also tell them that their hearing, seeing, feeling, and other sensory abilities are intact. Their intelligence is OK. They are like an expensive Mercedes with an empty tank. They have a lack of Serotonin in their brain. With antidepressant medication, we will fill that empty tank. The Mercedes will run well again.

My patients are able to separate themselves from the pervasive feeling of uselessness and focus on their treatment. They are like a Mercedes car with an empty gas tank.

ANTIDEPRESSANTS VS. TRANQUILIZERS AND HYPNOSIS IN THE TREATMENT OF DEPRESSION

When you go for the treatment of an infection in your throat, your doctor gives you antibiotics to kill the germs, Tylenol for headaches and fever, and cough syrup for a cough.

It takes few days before the antibiotic has killed enough germs to control your fever and cough. Until then you keep taking your Tylenol and cough syrup. Once you have no more fever, you stop taking the Tylenol and cough syrup. However, you continue to take your antibiotic full course. This prevents the infection from coming back and prevents development of resistance to treatment.

Let's say that I am starting you on three medications to treat your Depression/panic disorder/OCD.

Sertraline is a medication to treat depression, panic attacks, and OCD. Alprazolam is a tranquilizer to calm anxiety. Zolpidem is a sleeping pill.

Like the antibiotic for a sore throat, Sertraline is the real medicine which is going to treat your illness. It takes time, like the antibiotic, to reach the roots of depression. It is slow but steady. You continue taking it even if you start feeling better to avoid the return of the illness and to prevent future attacks of depression from becoming resistant to treatment.

Alprazolam and Zolpidem are for anxiety and sleeplessness. As soon as the depression lifts, your anxiety and sleep may become better. You will not need them except once in a while.

Recommended Reading

BOOKS

Aesop, Vernon Jones, V. S., & Rackham, Arthur. (1992). *AESOP'S FABLES* (first edition ed.): Avenel Books.

American Psychiatric Association., & American Psychiatric Association. DSM-5 Task Force. (2013). *Diagnostic and statistical manual of mental disorders : DSM-5* (5th ed.). Washington, D.C.: American Psychiatric Association.

Angelo, C. (1981). The Use of Metaphoric Objects in Family Therapy. *American Journal of Family Therapy, 9*(69-78).

Bandler, Richard, & Grinder, John. (1979). *Frogs into princes : neuro linguistic programming*. Moab, Utah: Real People Press.

Barker, P. (1983). *Basic Child Psychiatry* (4 ed.). London: Granada, and Baltimore: University Park Press.

Barker, P (1981). Paradoxical Techniques in Psychotherapy. In D. S. Freeman & B. Trute (Eds.), *Treating Families with Special Needs*. Ottawa: Canadian Association of Social Workers.

Bettelheim, Bruno. (1977). *The uses of enchantment: the meaning and importance of fairy tales*. New York: Vintage Books.

Burns, George W. (2001). *101 Healing Stories: Using Metaphors in Therapy* (Ist ed.): John Wiley & Son.

Chalmers, Robert. (2007). *The Jataka* (Vol. 1 & 2): Forgotten Books.

Close, Henry T. (1998). *Metaphor in Psychotherapy: Clinical Applications of Stories and Allegories (Practical Therapist)*: Impact Publishers

Dilts, R., Grinder, J., Bandler, R., Bandler, L.C., & DeLozier, J. (1980). *Neuro-linguistic Programming Volume I*. Cupertino, California: Meta Publications.

Erickson, M. H. (1980a). *Hypnotic Alteration of Sensory, Perceptual and Psychological Processes*. New York: Irivington.

Erickson, M. H. (1980b). *Hypnotic Investigation of Psychodynamic Processes*. New York: Irivington.

Erickson, M. H. (1980c). *Innovative Psychotherapy*. New York: Iriivngton.

Erickson, M. H. (1980d). *A Teaching Seminar with Milton H. Erickson, M.D.* New York: Brunner/Mazel.

Erickson, M. H. (1980). *The Nature of Hypnosis and Suggestion*. New York: Irvington.

Erickson, M. H., Rossi, E.L., & Rossi, S. I. (1976). *Hypnotic Realities*. New York: Irvington.

Gordon, D. (1978). *Therapeutic Metaphors*. Cupertino, California: Meta Publications.

Haley, J. (1973). *Uncommon Therapy: The Psychiatric Techniques of Milton H. Erickson, M.D.* New York: Norton.

Haley, J. (1976). *Problem-Solving Therapy*. San Francisco: Jossey-Bass.

Johnson, Spencer. (1998). *Who moved my cheese?: an amazing way to deal with change in your work and in your life*. New York: Putnam.

Kopp, Richard R. (1995)). *Metaphor Therapy: Using Client Generated Metaphors In Psychotherapy* Routledge.

Rosen, S. (Ed.). (1982). *My Voice Will Go With You: The Teaching Tales of Milton H. Erickson, M.D.* New York: Norton.

Siegelman, Ellen Y. (1993). *Metaphor and Meaning in Psychotherapy* The Guilford Press

Tay, Dennis. (2013). Metaphor in Psychotherapy: A descriptive and prescriptive analysis (Metaphor in Language, Cognition, and Communication) (pp. 219): John Benjamins Publishing Company.

Turbayne, C. M. (1970). *The Myth of Metaphor*. Columbia, South Caroline: University of South Carolina Press.

Zeig, J. (1980). *In M. H. Erickson, A Teaching Seminar With Milton H. Erickson, M. D.* New York: Brunner/Mazel.

INTERNET RESOURCES

Cognitive Behaviour Therapy Self-Help Resources, Get Self Help. http://www.get.gg/index.html.

Mastering the Metaphor, ACBS World Conference IX, Colleen Ehrnstrom, Ph.D., Boulder, Colorado, USA. http://contextualscience.org/system/files/Mastering_The_Metaphor_ Ehrnstrom.pdf.

Daniel Eckstein—Six Types of Counseling Metaphors. www.alfredadler.org/.../eckstein%20sixtypescounselingmetaphorspp.ppt.

Metaphors in the therapeutic encounter—Cruse Bereavement Care. http://www.cruse.org.uk/sites/default/files/default_images/pdf/Events/Creative%20methods%20Metaphor%20inn%20Psychotherapy.pdf.

Psychology Tools. http://www.psychologytools.org/metaphor.html.

Therapeutic Metaphor. http://www.therapeuticmetaphors.com/.

Visual metaphors—Accept and Change. http://www.acceptandchange.com/visual-metaphors/.

METAPHOR THERAPY—YouTube. www.youtube.com/watch?v=ev3RYZOyZjA.

Milton H. Erickson—Wikipedia, the free encyclopedia. en.wikipedia.org/wiki/Milton_H._Erickson.

Index

absolute words, 149
abusive relationships, 102–103, 158
achievement, failure and, 58
acne, 37–38
addiction, 112, 171–174; complement,
    30–31
advice, giving, 26–27, 35, 145, 149, 152
aging spouse, 77–78
airplanes, 101, 120
alarm clock, 101–102
alcoholics, 112
alertness, 7–8
anger, 24–25, 26, 50–51, 97–98, 148,
    165–166, 169–170; emotional outlet
    replacing, 155–156; impulsive actions
    resulting from, 99–100; luxury of
    working through, 28–29; XYZ
    approach to, 154
antidepressants, 179–180
antidote thoughts, 59
apartment, relationship as, 164
apologies, 155
appearance, judging by, 147
apples, 164
April showers, 123
arguments, 27, 32, 54, 153–154; avalanche
    in, 157; chicken-egg, 161; over
    complement, 150; pyramid metaphor,
    164–165
arrest, 81
asking, for help, 146–147

assertiveness, 147–148, 150, 152
assumption monster, 36–37
attic, 76, 79–80
avalanche, 157

babysitter, 5–6
backseat drivers, 21
backup generator, 5–6
bad habits, 96
bad moods, 29–30, 146
ball, trampoline and, 54
ball of clay, 110
ballpoint pens, 22
bananas, 16–17, 162
barber, 108
basketball game, 115
bathroom, 10
bathtub, 142
bats, 11
beads, necklace, 25
beggar, prince and, 5
behavior: according to situations, 2; French
    fries and, 68; GPS model for, 26–27;
    spending, 10–11, 138
best friend, 87
bills, 87
binge drinking, 171
birds, 125–126, 133
blinders, on racehorse, 8–9
blisters, 134–135
blossoms, plucking, 31

blueprint, house and, 120
boats, 7, 169
body parts, loss of, 131
bogeyman, 60
boulders, 44, 54–55
boxing, 152–153
brain, 12, 100–101, 149
brakes, cars with defective, 20
bricks, on muddy path, 49–50
bridges, 19, 75
broken glass, 26
broken taillight, 47
bucket of water, on campfire, 99–100
bullets, 151
bumpy road, 116, 127
bunny, rattlesnake and, 2
burn-out, 98
burs, 62
butter, 51, 107, 146–147
butterfly, caterpillar and, 112

cab, 91–92
cactus flower, 160–161
caffeine, 172
calculator, brain as, 149
campfire, 99–100
candles, 173
car accident, 34–35
cards, playing, 44
cars, 4, 20, 34–35, 84, 159–160; changing
    spouses and, 158; idling engine of, 62;
    importance of all parts of, 145–146;
    passing, 12–13; safe distance between,
    23–24; steering emotions and, 57–58;
    trading in, 165
caterpillar, butterfly and, 112
cauliflower, rose *vs.*, 85
cause & effect, 139
cave, light in dark, 64
centipede, 131
change, being bothered by, 134
cheating, on spouse, 169
chemicals, 33–34
cherries, 19
chewing gum, emotional, 66
chicken-egg argument, 161
Christmas tree, 20–21
cigarettes, 15–16
clay ball, 110

clock, alarm, 101–102
clutter, 6, 9, 48–49, 76, 111–112
coal mine, 120–121
coats, hook holding too many, 167
cocoons, 22–23, 112
coins, 27–28, 36
coloring book, 3
commands, 113
communication, 29–30; phone, 30; you
    said I heard, 20–21
complainers, 65–66
complements, 30–31, 150, 152
concentration camps, 45
connecting dots, 129–130
conscience, bad neighbor-like, 132–133
consideration, for others, 145–156;
    everyone as important, 145–146; good
    for one, bad for other, 148; I say it as it
    is view, 150; judging by appearance,
    147; opinions and, 151; over-
    sharpening and assertiveness in,
    147–148; speaking truthfully, 152–153
cookie cutters, 72–73, 87–88
cooking spaghetti, 93–94
counterfeit coins, 27–28
cracked eggs, 134
credit cards, 40, 111
crises, 53, 86
criticism, 18–19, 83–84, 90, 154–155
cross-contamination, in marriage issues,
    161
cushioned stickers, 135–136

dandelions, 132
darkness, 45, 64, 141
dating, 91–94; as cooking spaghetti,
    93–94; loneliness and, 93; rejection in,
    93
days, 3, 11, 77, 110; feeding to past, 70; as
    ordinary masterpieces, 3–4
dead donkey, 76
dead ends, 139
deadlines, 121
debit card, 111
debts, 40
decisions, wrong, 96
decorating, 3, 8
defective brakes, 20
depression, 141, 176–177, 179, 179–180

desert, 73–74, 160–161
diamonds, 37, 82, 120–121, 123, 124
difficult patients. *See* patients, connecting
    with difficult
dimmers, light, 23
dingy boat, 7
disabled woman, 59–60
distractions, 8–9
divorce, 16–17
doctors, 178–179
dogs, 24
donkey, dead, 76
dots, connecting, 129–130
drama, 102
dreamhouse, 120
dreaming big, 122
drinking, 171
driving, 3, 4–5, 7–8, 21, 176
drowning, in bathtub, 142
duck, 58
DUI, 81, 99
dung, 75

earthmover, 125
earwax, 143
echo, 6–7, 107–108
economics, emotional, 25–26
Edison, Thomas Alva, 125
education, 120, 120–121, 124, 124–125
eggs, 134, 161
email, 59
emotions, 6, 52, 140–141; anger outlet
    through, 155–156; chewing gum and,
    66; economics and, 25–26; emotional
    flu, 147; emotional tailgating, 34–35;
    healing blemishes on, 37–38; steering,
    57–58; talking about, 177; ticks and,
    48; universal, 85
encouragement, 18–19
engine, 10, 62; fire, vii
epilepsy seizures, 50
evaporated water, 154
exits, highway, 121
expectations, 167

failure, achievement and, 58
falling, 71–72, 122
family, 9
farmer, 106

fault-finding, 97
fear, 63, 67; of medication side-effects,
    175; of rejection, 71–72, 137–138
feedback, 100, 153
feelings, courage to feel, 78
file it away concept, 111–112
financial hardships, 46, 49–50, 53
fire engine, vii
fish, 54, 126
flat tires, 46, 148
flies, 97, 133
floating, 86
flowerbed, 41
flowers, 130–131, 137–138, 138
flying, 72, 101, 125–126
food, saving, 78–79
forest fire, 169–170
foundation, building strong, 100–101
framed page, from coloring book, 3
French fries, 68
friends and friendships, 37, 98–99, 135;
    abandoned gold mines and, 18; acid
    words in, 33–34; ballpoint pens as, 22;
    best, 87, 104; counterfeit, 27–28;
    earthmover-snake, 125; help during
    crisis from strong, 86; out of touch, 18;
    tree of, 28. *See also* interpersonal
    relationships
frightening mask, 163
front lawn, 71
frozen butter, 51
frugality, misplaced, 78
fun, 1–2

garage sales, 86, 86–87
garbage, 18, 100
gasoline, 26, 77, 97–98, 173, 173–174, 179
gas station, 103
generator, backup, 5–6
germs, 165–166
gifts, 77, 159
glass, broken, 26
goals, 120, 124–125
golden opportunities, 124
gold mines, 18
gorilla, 36–37
GPS, 2, 7, 26–27
grief, 28–29
guests, 103–104

guilt, 101
gum, emotional chewing, 66

habits, 55, 96, 99
hands, 114–115
happiness, 95–112; balanced life for, 96–97; changing work for, 95; doing what brings, 64; drama and, 102; guilt and, 101; honey bee and house fly metaphor, 97; king's concern with everyone's, 119–120; strong foundation for, 100–101; talent and success in, 95–96; video collection of memories for, 105; worry leeches and, 97
happy people, 5
head: getting out of, 74; guests in, 103–104; keeping unkind opinions in, 151; thoughts stored in, 61
headaches, 42
heart, 60, 163
helicopter landing, 24
help, asking for, 146–147
heroin, 30–31
highway of life, 4–5, 11, 117, 118, 121; emotional tailgating on, 34–35; overheated engine on, 10; staying alert on, 7–8; thoughts veering off from, 77–78; unplanned exits on, 121
hikers, 146
hobbies, 8–9
hobo guests, 103–104
home, 12
honey bee, 97
honking, 146
horses, 122, 132
hotel rooms, 32–33, 92–93
house fly, 97
houses, 92, 120, 169
hugs & kisses stage, 107
hurdles, self-made, 88–89
hurricane watch, 46–47
husband, ideal, 158–159
hypochondria, 176

ice cubes, 27
ideas, eggs as, 134
image, projected, 2
in between situations, 82
inferiority, 85

ingrown toenail, 139–140
injury, train tracks and, 110
insecurity, 63–64
insomnia, 111–112
interpersonal relationships, 15–38; anger and gasoline in, 26; assumption monster in, 36–37; attending to plants and, 33; broken glass, 26; cherries and, 19; complements and addictions, 30–31; counterfeit, 27–28; friendship rejuvenation, 18; healing emotional blemishes in, 37–38; ideal parents, 22–23; inner and outer work in, 17; lawn focus in, 31–32; losers in, 35–36; luxury of staying angry, 28–29; misunderstood encouragement in, 18–19; necklace beads and string metaphor, 25; orange cone metaphor, 29–30; plucking blossoms in, 31; punching bag scenario in, 16; reevaluation of past, 16–17; safe distance between cars, 23–24; sales call metaphor, 17; tantrums in, 29; termites as resentments in, 20; tree of friendship, 28; you said I heard communication issues in, 20–21. *See also* marriage
interviews, open-ended, vii–viii
I pay my bills attitude, 87
irritating remarks, 26
I say it as it is attitude, 150

jail cell, 8
job. *See* work
journey, 126, 139
judging, by appearance, 147
juicy mango, 113–114
jungle, 35
junk car, 159–160
junk mail, 59

key, new, 46
king, story of, 119–120
knives, 147–148, 152
knowledge, light of, 63

lake, 12, 135
lanes, highway, 4–5, 11, 117, 118
lateness, 50
lawns, 31–32, 71

leadership, 123
learning, 120–121, 126
leaves, 40–41
leeches, 97
left lane, on highway of life, 11, 121
letting go, living now, 69–80; aging spouse
    worry, 77–78; bag of memories, 78;
    bridge crossing and, 75; can't fly
    feeling, 72; days as gifts, 77; dead
    donkey from past, 76; fallen in well,
    71–72; feeding day to past, 70; getting
    out of head, 74; life at 30, 50 and 80,
    80; living is your business view, 70;
    living what can be controlled, 70;
    memory deadbolt lock, 72; misplaced
    frugality, 78; nasty remarks and, 79;
    orange slice and, 71; pain of past, 71;
    perpetuating own misery, 75; precious
    moments and, 73–74; saving food until
    spoiled, 78–79; unpleasant memories,
    79; veering off road, 77–78; visiting *vs.*
    living in past, 69
light, 64; dimmers, 23; of knowledge, 63
light bulb, 89
lion, mosquito and, 67
listening, 25–26
loneliness, 93
lone zebra, herd *vs.*, 42–43
looping, thought, 66
losers, 35–36
love, fear-based, 63
lucky mindset, 142
luxury, anger as, 28–29

mail, junk, 59
makeup, 104–105
mango, 113–114
manners, 135–136
maple tree, 90
maps, 121–122
marriage, romantic relationships and,
    157–170; acid words and chemicals,
    33–34; apples and pairs, 164; best gift,
    159; cheating in, 169; chicken-egg
    argument in, 161; cross-contamination
    of issues in, 161; expectations in, 167;
    expensive house ruining, 169; fear-
    based love in, 63; helicopter landing
    and, 24; hugs & kisses to hi & bye, 107;

hurt person not relationship, 162–163;
    ideal husband, 158–159; masks and,
    163; mommy is mad scenario in,
    161–162; oil change and maintenance
    in, 160; spoiled bananas of difficult,
    162; too much salt and work in, 108;
    trading in, 165; worry over aging
    spouse, 77–78. *See also* arguments
mashed potatoes, 68
masks, 163
matchbox, addiction as, 173
matchsticks, 10–11, 72
meals, 137
medication: depression, 179–180; desire to
    stop, 177; dosage, 177; fear of side-
    effects from, 175; patients seeking new,
    178–179; request to reduce, 178; self-
    medicating, 171
meditation throne, 10
memories, 69–70, 72, 78, 79–80, 80, 135;
    as dried rose petals, 109; soothing, 65;
    unpleasant, 79; video collection of, 105
menu, religion as restaurant, 82
Mercedes Benz, 84, 179
messages, nonverbal, 102–103
metaphors, usefulness of, vii–viii
middle ground, 48–49
millionaire, 117
mind, 7
mindset, 129–143; acceptance of change,
    134; bad neighbor conscience,
    132–133; cause & effect, 139;
    centipede, 131; choosing memories,
    135; connecting dots, 129–130; cracked
    eggs, 134; dandelions, 132; deciding
    what to look for, 136; flies as thoughts,
    133; flower bouquet, 130–131; journey
    and dead ends, 139; lucky, 142; no one
    is perfect, 138; problem or pleasure,
    136–137; random thought replacement,
    135; self-criticism, 139–140; stand-up
    toy, 131; surfer, 142; university of life,
    129; walk away clean, 140; walking
    with blisters, 134–135; what-if, 139;
    wild horses as thoughts, 132
misery, perpetuating own, 75
mistakes, 13, 48, 81
money, 10–11, 35–36, 138
monster, assumption, 36–37

moods, bad, 29–30, 146
mosquito, lion and, 67
mother meal, 137
motorist, stranded, 52
muddy path, bricks on, 49–50
mugger, 174
multiple choices, recognizing, 49

Narcan injections, 59
nasty remarks, 79
negative thinking, 57–68, 141; antidote
    thoughts, 59; complainers and, 65–66;
    doing what brings happiness, 64;
    French fries and, 68; getting out of own
    way, 60; insecurity and, 63–64; light of
    knowledge for, 63; love based on fear
    and, 63; magnifying problems and, 67;
    playing thoughts actively, 64; quality
    control and, 66–67; soothing memories
    for, 65; spoken words as eggs approach
    to, 61–62; tangled burs and, 62; weed
    pulling for reducing, 67–68; what ifs
    and, 57
neighbor, bad, 132–133
new relationships, 18, 37
night, 45
nonverbal messages, 102–103
nose, 12
nuts and bolts story, 167–168

octopus, turtle and, 109
office, problems in home and, 12
oil change, 160
one-way street, 154–155
open-ended interview, vii–viii
open windows, 59–60
opinions, 51, 87–88, 113, 114–115; eggs
    as, 134; unkind, 151
opportunities, 119, 124
oranges, 71, 147
ordinary masterpiece, 3–4
organizations, 114–115, 123
oven, 107
overcoats, 167
overheated engine, 10

pace, of life, 117
pain, of past, 71
papers, 125–126; as flying bats, 11

parents, ideal, 22–23
past, 18, 76; feeding day to, 70; new
    relationships and, 18; pain of, 71;
    reevaluating, 16–17; visiting *vs.* living
    in, 69
patients, connecting with difficult,
    175–180; depression lifting in time,
    176–177; desire to stop taking
    medication, 177; emotional talk, 177;
    fear of side-effects, 175; helping to
    open, 175; hopelessness and
    hopefulness, 179; hypochondria, 176;
    seeking new doctor and medication,
    178–179. *See also* medication
Paycheck, Johnny, 7
pebbles, 44, 135
peeling potatoes, vii
penny tossing, 117
perfectionism, 138
personality, 47, 88, 104–105
pest problems, 62
phone, 30
photo album of life, 69–70
photocopy, of day, 3
pictures, 8, 36–37, 67
piece of paper, 125–126
pigsty, 153–154
pillow fight, 32
pizzeria, exclusive restaurant *vs.*, 91
planning, 47–48, 124–125, 127
plants, 9, 23, 33, 159
playing cards, 44
plucking blossoms, 31
polishing diamonds, 124
potatoes, vii, 68
potted Christmas tree, 20–21
power walk, 4
precious moments, 73–74
prince, beggar and, 5
priorities, 8, 42–43, 169
problems: earwax and, 143; as flat tires,
    46; ignoring or handling, 39–40;
    magnifying, 67; pest, 62; as rat
    droppings, 40; snakes as pleasures or,
    136–137; surfer view of, 142; task
    prioritizing, 42–43; universal nature of,
    51. *See also* financial hardships
problem-solving, 39–55; boulder in path
    metaphor, 54–55; dark night and, 45;

emotional ticks, 48; headache metaphor, 42; for others and self, 52; plane, convex or concave surfaces in, 39; plan for road crossing, 47–48; puddles and, 49; recognizing potential, 46–47; simple solutions for complex problems, 50; stones in path and, 41; sunshine-clothesline metaphor, 44–45; task prioritizing, 42–43; this-or-that trap, 45; turn-around reactions, 40–41; umbrella metaphor, 142; worrying compared to, 41–42

procrastination, 114

professional burn-out, 98

professional hikers, 146

projected image, 2

pruning, 9

psychoanalysis, 41

psychological attic, 79–80

public relations manager, 100

puddles, 6, 49, 122

punching bag, 16

pyramid, 164–165

quality time, 158

quiet place, 10

quitting, job, 7

racehorse blinders, 8–9

rain, 123

raindrops, 64–65

rat droppings, 40

rattlesnake, bunny and, 2

razor sharp knives, 152

real estate agent, acting like, 83–84

real self, 82–83

recipes, doctors as chefs with, 178–179

rejection, 72–73, 85, 93; fear of, 71–72, 137–138

relationships: abusive, 102–103, 158; banana metaphor for ending relationships, 16–17; cigarettes and, 15–16; contributions in, 116; emotional ticks as problematic, 48; flower bouquet and ended, 130–131; as jungles, 35; keeping safe distance in, 23–24; light dimmers metaphor for modifying, 23; middle ground in, 48–49; nonverbal messages in, 102–103; not neglecting,

146; perfectionism and, 138; polishing new, 37; problems in, 51; ripped sofa metaphor for problems in, 39–40; as rose blossoms, 136; tired of apartment or, 164; too much salt in, 108; transitory, 32–33; as two-sided coins, 36; valuing present, 105–106; as windows, 26. *See also* interpersonal relationships; marriage, romantic relationships and

religion, 82

resentment, 165–166

restaurants, 82, 91

retirement, 5

rich farmer, 106

road, 116, 140–141; dead end, 139

road map, 117–118

road metaphors, 47–48, 127

romantic relationships. *See* marriage, romantic relationships and

rose bushes, 90, 98–99

roses, 85, 109, 136

roses and thorns, 22, 29, 30, 37, 103, 152

rushing, 4

sales, 17. *See also* garage sales

salt, 96–97, 101, 108

sand castle, 124–125

sarcasm, 24–25

scenic route, 2

screwdrivers, 85

secrets, keeping, 154

seizures, epilepsy, 50

self, 85, 88; accepting mistakes, 81; being true to, 89–90; as best friend, 87; garage sales wisdom, 86, 86–87; grabbing a log to float, 86; help from strong friends, 86; inferiority, 85; knowing and appreciating, 81–90; others' opinions of, 87, 87–88; read estate agent promotion of, 83–84; real, 82–83; recognizing strengths and weaknesses of, 85; in between situations of, 82; strengths and weaknesses of, 90; warts and, 81

self-criticism, 88–89, 139–140

self-improvement, 95–112; anger and impulsiveness lesson for, 99–100; anger energy used for, 97–98; applying

makeup to personality for, 104–105; bad habits and, 96; being own public relations manager for, 100; wrong decisions and, 96
self-medicating, 171
self-talk, 4
shoes, 166–167, 178
shopkeepers, 89–90
side-effects, fear of, 175
skyscraper, 124–125
snakes, 2, 35, 55, 95, 96, 125, 136–137, 146
snow, 40–41, 43–44, 137–138
soap dispensers, 35
sobriety, addiction and, 173–174
sofa, 104
sofas, 39–40
son, mother's criticism of, 83–84
soothing memories, 65
sound maker, white noise, 83
spaghetti, 93–94
Spanish proverb, 154–155
speaking truthfully, 152–153
spending money, 10–11, 138
spoiled bananas, 162
spoken words, actions as eggs hatching from, 61–62
spouses, 77–78, 158, 158–159, 166; cheating on, 169
stand-up toy, 131
statues, 82–83, 105–106
steer dung, 75
steering emotions, 57–58
stickers, manners as cushioned, 135–136
stones, in path, 41
store windows, 88, 89–90
storms, surviving, 53
stranded motorist, 52
stress, 10, 50, 83
success, working toward, 113–127; changing lanes and, 118; leadership and, 123; planning and, 127; procrastination and, 114; unexpected results of, 113–114; unplanned exits and missed deadlines, 121
sugar, 155, 168–169
sugarcoating, 153
suggestions, as orders, 145
sunshine, 44–45, 89

surfaces, plane, convex or concave, 39
surfer mindset, 142
swan, 12
swimming pool, 98, 166

tailgating, 34–35
taillight, broken, 47
talent, 122–123, 123
talents, 95–96
tantrums, 29
tea kettle, 50–51
termites, 20
this-or-that trap, 45
thorns. *See* roses and thorns
thoughts: actively playing enjoyable, 64; all minds having similar, 12; antidote, 59; as birds, 133; fear of bad, 67; flies as, 133; hatching eggs and, 106; heart as believing, 60; looping, 66; quality control of, 66–67; replacing, 135; steering emotions and, 57–58; stored in head, 61; strange, 12; unwanted, 59; veering off of, 77–78; as wild horses, 132. *See also* negative thinking
throne, meditation, 10
ticks, 48, 99
tires, 46, 148, 165
toenail, ingrown, 139–140
toes, 48, 151
toilet paper, 140
toilet seat, 10
tomato sauce, marriage and zesty, 168–169
tornadoes, 123
tourists, 1
traffic, 12–13
train tracks, 110
trampoline, 54
tranquilizers, 179–180
trap, this-or-that, 45
trash, 86–87
treasure, 86–87
trees, 28, 90
turn-around reactions, to problems, 40–41
turtle, octopus and, 109

umbrella, 116–117, 142
unhappy people, 5
university of life mindset, 129
unspoken words, 146

vacations, 9

vase, heart as, 163

vice president, misplaced frugality of, 78

videos, viii; memories and, 105

walking, 4, 31, 115, 134–135, 140

warm hands, 114–115

warts, 81

water, 73–74, 99–100, 135, 154

water lily, fish and, 54

waves of sea, 119, 142

weeds, pulling, 67–68

weight loss, 43

wells, 6–7, 71–72, 141

what ifs, 57, 139

white noise, 83

wild horses, 132

windows, 26, 59–60, 88, 89–90, 140–141

winter, 74–75

withdrawal, anger expressed as, 170

words: absolute, 149; acid, 33–34; bullets of unkind, 151; eggs hatching from

spoken, 61–62; unspoken, 146

work, 1–13; burn-out, 98; changing, 95; clutter and, 9; dingy boat metaphor, 7; file it away concept for undone, 111–112; giving 100% to, 116–117; inner and outer, 17; job as left lane of life, 121; job interviews, 172; quitting job, 7; too much salt as too much, 108; umbrella at, 116–117

world, as hollow well, 6–7

worry, 41–42, 43–44, 62, 66, 74–75, 77–78, 97; yelling out of, 151

wrong decisions, 96

XYZ, approach to anger, 154

yelling, 30, 149, 151

zebra, 42–43

zipper, 154